THE RELUCTANT PILGRIM

THE RELUCTANT PILGRIM

VOL. I: ASHES AND ASCENT

TRANCE BLACKMAN

First Edition, 2024
Published by Entranced Studios

The Reluctant Pilgrim, Vol. I: Ashes and Ascent ISBNs:

978-0-9734758-2-1   Hardcover
978-0-9734758-1-4   Paperback
978-0-9734758-3-8   ePub
978-0-9734758-4-5   PDF
978-0-9734758-6-9   Audiobook

Entranced Studios

CONTENTS

INTRODUCTION

The Reluctant Pilgrim, Vol. I: Ashes and Ascent features writings from May 2015 to December 2016. In 2019, I revisited, revised, and updated my published online work, refining some pieces to make them more evergreen while removing those that no longer reflected my beliefs, perspectives, or philosophy.

In 2024, I began anew, preparing for this book's publication. As of this writing, all chapters in this book are also available on my website — tranceblackman.com.

The Reluctant Pilgrim is a journey through the labyrinth of self-discovery, creativity, and spiritual awakening. Blending poetry, poetic musings, reflective essays, and provocative prose, it invites readers to explore vulnerability, personal growth, and the dynamic interplay between impulse and action.

You may notice some repetition of ideas and themes. This, as I'm sure you'd agree, is part of the process. With most reading, research, or study, we often find revelations and unexpected inspiration in the familiar. Repetition can serve as a tool for penetrating preconceptions, challenging long-held beliefs, and shifting our personal worldview, especially when exploring alternative, thought-provoking, or uncommon perspectives.

This book is my heartfelt offering to seekers, dreamers, and those yearning to align with their most authentic selves. Through reflections on love, musings on the nature of reality, and sparks of creative passion, I hope *The Reluctant Pilgrim* illuminates a path toward greater understanding, connection, and fulfillment.

Thank you for joining me on this journey.

Trance Blackman
December, 2024

SOLITUDE

As artists
We love alone
Abhor lonely
Lonely implies a disconnect
From the source
The stream of inspirations
The pulse of the creative
Alone is
Universal
A unity
A space
To gather the nuances
To dance with the flow
Lonely is forgetting
A self-imposed punishment
A discoloration and
False
Alone
We are all one

VULNERABILITY

Vulnerability is the silent doorway to everything we desire yet often fear. In a world obsessed with strength and control, it feels risky to let down our guard — but it is only through this unguarded state that we truly connect, heal, and grow.

. . .

Vulnerability is a tricky thing. We live in a society with ambiguous ideas about strength, power, and courage — a society that often subsists on basic impulses, emotional bargaining, manipulation, and psychological underdevelopment.

As adults, vulnerability is particularly challenging. We strive for confidence, projecting an air of strength, balance, control, and availability. Yet, we tend to equate vulnerability with weakness — that's the catch. Preconceived ideas about how relationships should look and how we want to be perceived create a fog of noise, rendering us ineffective when things get tough. Truth and character will always surface, no matter how much we subdue, suppress, edit, or try to hide behind guilt, shame, anger, blame, and other coping mechanisms. Left unchecked, these only lead to mental and physical health issues.

Many of us have endured various forms of pain, leaving a deep part of us unfulfilled, especially in matters of love. This often results in struggles with adulthood, as we stumble and collide with each other across all aspects of society, desperate for connection but fearful of rejection and judgment.

Collectively, it would seem we are awakening. Today, the exploration of dualities — the yin and yang, right and wrong, masculine and feminine — is quite prevalent. Widespread protests, social activism, the information age, and the exposure of hidden truths all push us to shatter outdated paradigms. As a species, we are always integrating everything that has come before, the unwavering impulse to release darkness through acceptance, and creating space for powerful intentions to take root. Vulnerability is at the core of this shift.

We've all been hurt — perhaps deeply — and fear getting hurt again. So, do we isolate, retreat, hibernate, avoid risks, and settle for a lesser version of ourselves? That might protect us temporarily, but life relentlessly pushes on. It refuses to stagnate. Living as a mere shadow of ourselves only reinforces feelings of emptiness, a lack of vitality, and a heartbreaking loss of motivation — especially when it comes to pursuing what excites and fulfills us.

The true weapons of mass destruction have always been fear-based ideas and massive lies perpetuated by ancient forces within our realm. Yet more and more of us are realizing our true power through a deeper, heart-centered intelligence. Love knows. We know. We feel it. We embody it.

It starts — and it ends — within. Reignite your inner fire. Face the truth of who you are and who you may be pretending to be. Reconnect with your authentic self and embrace your unique story. As Matt Kahn says, "Whatever arises, love that." The time has come.

Vulnerability is the key.

Love your life

BETWEEN IMPULSE AND ACTION

What if there are no wrong turns, no wasted time, no missed chances? What if every step, every pause, every spark of curiosity is part of the design? Life doesn't demand perfection — it asks only for presence, for a willingness to step into the vast, uncharted space where stillness meets transformation.

. . .

There are no truly missed marks, lost opportunities, or wasted moments. Instead, there are choices, limitless possibilities, preferences, and perspectives. Every moment we allow ourselves to dance in the space between impulse and (re)action, observation and inquiry, is utterly perfect.

But we don't often inhabit that space, do we? What's missing?

Life is. Life hungers and craves. Life is an experience, and it adores everything about you. But what is life?

Life is not linear in time and space, even if we perceive it to be so. It isn't quantifiable, and our attempts to define it often diminish its essence. Life thrives in the spaces between labels and judgments, flourishing effortlessly and indefinitely, whether or not you believe it's working in any meaningful way for you.

It teases you with knowledge and awareness, foresight and hindsight, intuition, intention, and imagination. These are its invitations — tools to help you navigate and realign with your deepest truths.

Within you, your innermost being is a churning flow of energy, like molten lava in flux and excitement, anticipating the next breath, lesson, or step — ever the responsive collaborator.

What is learning? It's remembering, filtered through adaptation. The infinitesimal variations you encounter every dreaming, waking, and walking second favor your preconceptions. Yet even carved stone is malleable — after all, a stone is simply another form of vibration.

Life's scope and scale are immeasurable. Boundaries exist only within the level of understanding that created them. The mind seeks structure, but true freedom emerges when we treat it as a co-pilot, allowing the vastness of life to guide the ship.

Solvitur ambulando

VALUABLE

Just because something or someone is not currently available to you does not invalidate your desires or feelings. It's an opportunity for honest reflection and profound realization. Be grateful. Instead of berating, rejecting, abandoning, or denying what is fundamentally and powerfully good, honor yourself and what you value.

This is a safe place to begin a new journey.

You have healed something essential for the next phase of your life.

Solvitur ambulando

NOTES ON PRESENCE

Allow yourself to feel a bit of hunger, rather than constantly eating. Savor that first bite.

Allow yourself to crave a little, instead of pouring another glass out of habit.

Watch the effortless waves on the water, how they bend time in slow motion.

Listen to the snow compress beneath your boots.

Remember the anger, dread, worry, anxiety, stress, anticipation, revelation, emancipation, jubilation, elation; remember that it passed.

Remember when you were authentic and generous. Remember when you could have been more so. Then, let it go.

Allow yourself to know it will all work out.

Allow yourself to know there is nothing to fear.

Love your life

To Make an Omelette

When faced with choices that cause inner conflict, be willing to sit with and explore your true feelings honestly, moving your energy through creative or expressive outlets, so you can release illusions, stay aligned with your authentic self, and live with an open heart.

. . .

If you're conflicted about a relationship, career, life choice, or anything weighing on you — something that influences your decisions, causes stagnation, and makes you wince when others offer suggestions — be willing to sit with it, explore it, and define your reasoning, beliefs, and perceptions. You're at odds with your values.

Allow yourself to be completely broken open, honest, and profoundly authentic with yourself. Tears and primal screams may be in order. Drum circles, acting classes, martial arts, and dance lessons can also help. The goal is to shake things up, to move, channel, and utilize your energy — to create something meaningful.

It is futile to try keep everything together by pampering, protecting, and nurturing the illusion of a "functional" existence. Be willing to crack the egg. Notice when you've become overly critical of yourself — of who you are, what you do, and how you do it — and when this attitude extends to others. You may be skirting a larger issue, and it's time to listen closely to that still, small voice within. You'll harm yourself less, figuratively and literally.

Painting over your true feelings, settling for what doesn't feel right, or appeasing the opinions and expectations of others can harden your heart. You serve no one with a heart that is caged, tempered, or timid. Your truth will never allow you to settle for anything that isn't fully aligned with your soul.

Love your life

THE PURSUIT OF A PASSION

We often avoid pursuing our passions out of fear of failure, but the key is to start where we are, embrace the journey, and trust that simply being present is enough for growth and transformation.

. . .

I wonder... How many of us never truly take the chance to go for it — to pursue our passion (which, of course, can change) — because we're afraid of failing?

Perhaps it's because failing at the one thing (since we've reduced it to just one thing) we've always desperately wanted to be or do presents a conundrum: If we fail, then what?

Under these conditions, a part of us keeps it just out of reach, and our repetitive thoughts and habitual actions affirm it:

Oh, when I feel prepared... Must prepare, prepare, prepare.

Oh, when I can afford it... Must buy lottery tickets...

Oh, I can't make any money from it, so I'll have to make it a side hustle... Just get a normal job...

Oh, I can't make a good living from it, so who would want to date, love, or marry me? I'm not worthy...

Oh, I tried (a little) here and there over the years, but nobody seems to care...

Oh, when I can find the time... I despise my job because it drains all my energy and motivation. Everyone I work with is an idiot.

Oh, I wish I could... then I would finally... be... happy.

And so on.

We can be quite clever in our clamoring, but it's often much ado about nothing.

Just begin. Where you are, who you are, and what you have to work with is perfect — it could be no other way. It will change. Teachers will appear, and lessons will materialize. Opportunities will arise. Setbacks will happen. Life will sometimes suck. Along the way, you may discover something more aligned with your heart. You may inspire others with your courage, your experiences, your falls, and your successes. You might give up, feel exhausted, bored, frustrated, disoriented, or depressed.

So what?

All that proves is that you're alive.

Keep going. Move through it. Flow with it. And remember: you are not your thoughts or your feelings.

You are here, now. That matters. There are universal laws and infinitesimal details at work to ensure you exist exactly as you are. Simply being is enough.

Remember the adventure of it all. Dive in.

Love your life

Turning Pages

Every time you revisit a *past* chapter of your life, you have the opportunity to glean new wisdom relevant to the *present*.

You also have the opportunity to cut the ties that bind you to it and to let the winds carry it away.

It's your book.

Solvitur ambulando

Your Music

Don't hide. Don't pretend to be mediocre to fit in or to appease the terrified. They need your courage (to fail or succeed) to reconnect with or reawaken to their truth.

Be real. Be amazing. Let them criticize through green envy your red, gold, and white fires of passion.

[Be willing to] fall on your face, so to laugh as a creator in your elemental state.

Normalcy is a quiet death. You're not here to be a zombie.

Love your life

MASS CONSENSUS DISORDERS

*A mass consensus disorder refers to deeply ingrained societal beliefs
and frameworks — such as the importance of money, work, and
conflict — that are manipulated to maintain power and control, often
leading individuals to live in fear and denial of their true potential;
breaking free from these illusions requires reclaiming sovereignty and
embracing authenticity, despite the discomfort that change may bring.*

. . .

A *mass consensus disorder* is an idea, concept, endemic practice, or
framework deeply embedded in the culture, society, state, or nation
in which it thrives. It is absorbed through enculturation and
indoctrination, woven into an overarching narrative that influences
a population's values and priorities on multiple levels. While widely
practiced and accepted, any mass consensus can be manipulated
and exploited by those seeking power, profit, and control. For this
reason, adherence to it may cause profound harm, qualifying, in
my opinion, as a disorder.

Those who challenge a society's pervasive concepts and rules often
face ostracism or unreasonable hardship for choosing a path that
contradicts the prevailing zeitgeist — the defining spirit or mood of
an era, which is, more often than not, deliberately manufactured.

Some examples of mass consensus disorders in our time include:

- The importance of a well-paying job; wage slavery

- Government and paying taxes

- Economic growth; profit as priority

- Religion as dogma; needing to be saved; being born a sinner

- Love and hope as commodities

- Money as real and necessary; banking, debt, interest rates, inflation

- Real estate or vast material gains as an aspirational necessity

- Corporations as pillars of society

- The arts relegated to secondary or tertiary importance

- Earth and her resources treated as commodities

- Humanity's limitless spirit reduced to a commodity

- Struggle, chaos, violence, war, weapons, conflict, and competition normalized

- Love, unity, trust, passion, fulfillment, and joy treated as idyllic, unnatural, or rare

These, along with countless other ideas we may overlook or accept as givens, are often fabrications — lies we believe and perpetuate. We live in fear or quiet desperation, conditioned by a lifetime of mind control and social programming, afraid to truly thrive. This fear stems from an unwillingness to take responsibility for dismantling the familiar and creating something entirely new. So, we settle. We accept things as they are. Perhaps this is the wiser, more peaceful path, as resistance to entrenched systems inevitably generates friction, uncertainty, and social discord.

And yet, this way of living is but one possibility among countless others. What if we let the lies go? At first, we might lose our minds — which might not be such a terrible starting point. We wouldn't be able to accept the enormity of the change immediately. But as we begin to reclaim our sovereignty and clear the detritus lodged in our hearts and minds, the awakening will accelerate. The process will become easier. Our minds will clear, our thoughts will expand, and our hearts will guide us toward what is authentic and aligned with our true values.

This awakening is always happening, though more prominently in some areas of the world than others. Where you choose to live profoundly shapes your psychology and practiced philosophy. Change is constant, but most of us fail to notice the innumerable moving parts and adaptive structures endlessly reconfiguring and realigning.

You are in the game. You are vital. You're a catalyst, here for reasons only you can fully understand, experience, and explore. Don't let mass consensus disorders govern your reality. They are merely tools, as transient as anything else in this realm. You hold the power to accept or reject their influence. Always.

Quaerite veritatem

Perspectives

Your role is not to invalidate or question the path on the map of their journey. Your role is to understand your own perspective and what your perception of their choices stirs within you.

There is magic at play, beyond time and anything physical. Your role is to acknowledge and reintegrate it.

Everything outside of us is a reflection, a mirror of the ongoing exploration we engage in within. Our senses provide endless input and information, our emotions guide and gauge our spirit, and our awareness — our consciousness — is the ever-willing student and observer.

Love your life

STAGNATION

Energetic stagnation leads to mental and physical blockages, manifesting as pain, frustration, and disengagement. By trusting our inner calling, staying curious, and embracing the unknown, we can break free and create new, fulfilling momentum in life. We are conscious co-creators of our reality — always.

. . .

Stagnation often masquerades as obsessive behavior, much like escapism. When we limit our options in an ego-driven attempt to control or when we linger in a haze of indecision, we create blockages that inflame the physical body.

Everything is energy — vibration. Our reality depends on movement. Thoughts can influence matter, but matter must move. Thoughts, of course, never stop, and spacetime flows endlessly. When we construct roadblocks, speed bumps, or buffers to manage situations, we introduce resistance. That resistance often manifests as pain.

The challenge is learning to trust ourselves — to be honest, authentic, and vulnerable. Deep down, we always know our preferred path, our inner calling, our intuitive dreams and desires. But it's easy to get bogged down in the mundane, to make excuses — small ones at first, then larger ones, layering until we've built a dam to block the flow.

The results are unmistakable. Gratitude fades. We treat ourselves and others poorly. Tempers flare, defensiveness rises, shoulders hunch, aches and pains emerge, and even simple tasks feel overwhelming. We shut down, piece by piece.

In this state, we search for solutions — something extreme to break the internal stalemate. We crave aliveness. But to avoid further harm, we must address the underlying tension and its true source.

Releasing it doesn't require monumental effort. One small shift can spark momentum; one giant leap can carve a new path. Beyond these three-dimensional structures, a universe exists in the space between — the ethereal infinite — and it only knows *yes*.

At any moment, we can choose to remember the game. We can ask, *What if?* and *What else is possible?* We can re-engage with the mystery. Anticipation, excitement, and exhilaration return when we trust the process and take chances.

We can step forward, not out of desperation or scarcity, but with curiosity, wide eyes, and a quickened heartbeat. We strive not for fleeting gains but for fulfillment, upliftment, and alignment of spirit — heart and soul.

Desire is inherently destructive to the superficial. On some level, we will never truly entertain apathy or ennui. Stagnation is, ultimately, a momentary illusion.

Allow the artist to emerge. You are the reason it's called *conscious co-creation*.

Love your life

ELEVEN PERCENT

Significant societal change requires a critical mass of people to believe in or engage with new ideas. This influence is often shaped by mass media, social media, and cultural narratives that manipulate public perception through fear, distraction, and curated content. It is therefore essential for individuals to become aware of and reclaim the narrative that shapes their reality and collective future.

. . .

For meaningful change to occur, a certain percentage of the population must believe in it or, at the very least, form an opinion about it. Studies on tipping points, or critical mass, suggest it could be as little as 5% or as much as 10% or more.

Humans are powerful creators. Our thoughts are things. This creative force — whether applied locally, nationally, or across the world — can guide civilization toward enlightenment or darkness.

Consider the tactics used by those in positions of influence to manipulate public opinion and define our culture: mainstream media, politics, entertainment, religion, and education systems. The results are undeniable if you step outside the box of accepted normalcy and observe what's truly happening amid the noise.

Take the news, for example. Reports are synchronized locally, regionally, and nationally — even curated internationally. "Anchors" around the world repeat, almost word for word, the same "news" to audiences tuning in at the same time every day. It's an effective system for disseminating a unified message — one that shapes public discourse, feeds anxiety, and molds perspectives.

By design, the news is superficial, predominantly negative, visually unsettling, spiritually deflating, and mood-altering. Its purpose is to capture attention and infuse minds with distortions and illusions. One could argue it's an ingenious method for spreading falsehoods, instilling fear in subtle gradients, and shaping cultural narratives.

Simple ideas, when widely shared, act like slow, insidious poisons ingrained into our mental and emotional frameworks. In contrast, major events — like the aftermath of 9/11 — serve as blunt, powerful instruments to control the full spectrum of public perception. Together, these techniques create a dual-pronged system for influencing thought on both subtle and overt levels.

Today, social media amplifies this control. Algorithms aggressively curate your feed — a clever play on words, if ever there was one. Their sole purpose is to keep your eyes glued to the screen, swiping and scrolling endlessly between heartwarming distractions and fear-inducing content. The effect? A narrowing of perspective, a reshaping of values, and a continual reinforcement or alteration of opinions.

Much of what we believe about the nature of reality is suspect. Ten people can share the same experience and interpret it in ten different ways. So, which one is real? Which one is true?

How we perceive the world shapes it. What we focus on and believe in our hearts molds our experience of reality. It determines how we interact with others, the values we uphold, the decisions we make, the careers and relationships we choose, and what we teach and model for our children — even whether we decide to have children.

Awareness of the prevailing narrative is critical if we hope to rewrite it or shift its momentum. Will we recognize when we've reached a critical mass — say, 11%? Will we notice whether the ideas guiding us are truly our own, or if they've been quietly shaped by someone or something else?

Eyes open.

Solvitur ambulando

REWRITING OUR STORY

Rewriting our story is a challenging and transformative process. It is riddled with frustration and resistance as we confront outdated paradigms and acknowledge our role in creating this reality. Yet, true healing can only happen when we accept our past, embrace our full humanity, and reconnect with our hearts — moving beyond intellectualization and the distractions of the mind.

. . .

The process of rewriting our story is exhausting. Shadowy figures emerge from within, dragging struggle, anger, and denial to the surface as we work to uproot dysfunctional paradigms. Part of us rages because we feel we've been deceived for so long. Another part burns with impatience, unable to bear the pace of positive change, especially now, with awareness expanding and infusions of consciousness accelerating. The madness only deepens as we witness destructive actions continuing, amplifying our sense of powerlessness.

On this dynamic earthly plane, insanity thrives. Within the last century, we've come perilously close to destroying ourselves multiple times. And yet, we're continuously offered chances to let this old, repetitive story play out — to see if we might finally align with our greater truth and shift into a higher gear that propels this reality forward. But we resist our infinity.

Accepting reality as it is forms one part of the struggle. To truly engage with the mechanism of transformation, we must embrace everything we have been and accept the consequences of what we have not. The world is what it is, and profound healing can only occur when we turn to face our reflection. To integrate it all. To accept that every facet of this reality is part of our journey and, ultimately, our creation.

It's easy to lose ourselves in dissecting every nuance, trying to understand all the subtleties and motivations. But this quest for knowing is not the problem we think it is. It is a trap — a mental maze where the mind unravels endless threads, grasping for meaning, seeking justice, searching to relieve guilt and shame, and straining to bridge the chasm between the heart and the soul. There is no need.

We've been too caught up in the cerebral, lost in masculine logic, violence, and the spirals of intellectual distraction. Now is the time to release it all — to scream primal screams, cry rivers of truth, dance liberating dances, let go of illusions, and sit fully within our hearts.

We know. We've always known.

We created this.

Temet nosce

THE REBEL HEART

To live fully and authentically, we must embrace vulnerability, heal the emotional wounds and external noise that distort the wisdom of our hearts, and reconnect with the innate power and love within us. Every moment offers an opportunity for transformation.

. . .

Refuse to settle. A timid heart leads to tepid love, and tepid love benefits no one — not you, not your children, not the world. It's heartbreaking to witness and soul-crushing to live. Go for greatness. Give yourself permission to be extraordinary. But to be clear, this doesn't mean mimicking someone else you admire. Be your own kind of great, your own kind of extraordinary — and grow from there.

There is immense strength in vulnerability. Within it lie the seeds of trust.

The journey must begin within. A heart that is open and alive has the capacity to attract and hold profound love and miracles. Yet reaching beyond the constraints of socialization, past wounds, stigmas, and the shallow portrayals of love in popular media requires immense bravery and self-respect.

Harmful ideas corrupt the peace and innocence of the heart. Noise arises from broken relationships we see, endure, or inherit. It stems from spiritual suppression, cultural idiosyncrasies, shame, embarrassment, and guilt. But ultimately, it's just noise — borrowed stories, illusions, and remnants of the past.

We must be selective about the frequencies we allow into the sacred space of our hearts. Healing requires awareness of the toxins hidden in fragmented, misleading memories. Just as our bodies are constantly renewing themselves, health and vitality are the heart's natural state. Why wouldn't the heart also be capable of transformation? Though it exists in its own ethereal and energetic realm, the heart is the source of all good things — a permanent, bi-directional channel to the infinite.

Let go of emotional callousness. Soften.

Every moment presents an opportunity for change, even if small. Each step matters.

Honor what lives in your heart. Rekindle the hearth and stoke its eternal flame. Invite the dance of fire and passion back into your life. Reconnect with the infinite and divine.

You have it.
You are it.
Remember.

Love your life

Our Voice

Our voice is a unique and powerful expression of our being, shaping and reflecting our thoughts, emotions, and actions, and it is our responsibility to use it authentically, for it connects our past, present, and future, and influences the world around us.

. . .

Our voice. It's our style, our perspective, our reality, and, when we're in an authentic state, our note; a resonance unique to us across time and space.

It can alarm and agitate. It can heal or harm. It can calm and relax. It alters the state of mind, both within and without. It represents or misleads. It can focus, fragment, filigree, or fluster. It communicates both the conscious and the unconscious.

Our voice can find the path of least resistance, keep us present, reach deep into our being, distill truth, and touch the source.

It connects all of our stories, our histories — past, present, and future.

Our being is our voice. Our doing is our voice.

How we choose to speak, when to speak, with whom to speak, and why to speak — we choose to make noise, and we choose silence.

When it's important — when we're courageous, inspired, and ignited — with a deep breath, we stand and speak up.

When we defer to judgment, impatience, and fear — when we forget our power and reach instead for control — we talk down.

When we fall in love — when we embrace those foolish, life-affirming moments — with a quivering voice, we spill our guts and empty our trusting hearts.

With our voice, we sing, chant, incant, enchant, intone, inform, reform, emote, vote, and inspire. It is our signature. It is our identity, and it is our responsibility.

Our voice is our purpose and our expression. Our voice is our art, and it is an integral part of humanity's palette.

In whatever ways we choose to use it — to give it, to enjoy it, and to share it — we must use it, for no one has a voice just like ours.

Vox nostra, veritas nostra

LIGHTNESS OF BEING

Healing and wisdom emerge from authenticity and vulnerability —
letting go of old baggage, expanding our perspective, and aligning
with our hearts to welcome the growth and love life has to offer.

. . .

Our self-worth game can be messy, even cruel. Yet, when we
remain open to its lessons, those lessons become clear. It takes only
a shift in perspective.

Healing and understanding arise through authenticity and are
sustained by genuine vulnerability. Wisdom cannot be gained
without profound honesty — admitting what we don't know and
finding peace in that admission. This honesty invites curiosity, a
key that opens the door to deeper awareness.

To reach the higher level of consciousness required to unravel the
mystery of our being, we must first release the baggage that weighs
us down. By doing so, the spirit naturally rises. As perspectives shift
and perceptions broaden, an effortless, elevated attitude begins to
take shape, helping us see and understand truths we hadn't seen
before. In that process, we start to recognize how many of the
stories we've held onto are mere illusions.

In this newfound lightness of being, our gaze lifts to embrace an
entirely new horizon. With each step, we remember more of who
we truly are.

We learn as we grow, grow as we listen, and truly hear as we align
with our hearts.

Love your life

How We See the World

Our perception of reality is shaped by the filters we apply to the information we process. By shifting our perspective, we can transform our experience of the world.

. . .

Each day, we're exposed to an overwhelming amount of information — even carrying over into our sleep. We constantly select and filter the data we absorb, focusing on what aligns with our preferences or biases.

Consider how re-reading a book or re-watching a movie often reveals something new. Life is no different. Situations and challenges tend to reoccur, but unlike passive observers or entertained spectators, we are active participants. The difference lies in how we choose to engage.

What if, when familiar patterns repeat or old events replay in our minds, we could step back and view them with fresh eyes? What if we created a pause — a space between input and reaction — to allow for new insights to emerge?

The question often holds more power than the answer.

We can choose to see the world through cynical filters, focusing on chaos, violence, ignorance, and inequality. Or we can choose optimistic filters, seeing growth, innovation, peace, and greater harmony.

Same lenses, different filters — a different reality.

We decide. What if it really is that simple?

Solvitur ambulando

ANCHORS AND MOMENTUM

Every choice we make is both a stepping stone and a waypoint, initiating momentum toward our desires. While life's struggles and the underlying unease may feel overwhelming, they offer opportunities for growth, discernment, and transcendence within this unique, dynamic reality.

. . .

Each choice serves as both an anchor and a milestone on our journey — a potential point of stagnation or a foundation for growth. Every moment extends an invitation to begin anew. By following our excitement, we generate momentum that carries us closer to our desires.

Life's struggles are neither random nor meaningless. This reality is a space for creation through contrast, conflict, and limitation. We originate from an eternal source, and this world is our sandbox — a realm where challenges are meant to be experienced and transcended.

Death and destruction may appear real, but they are illusions. Beneath the surface of this chaotic realm lies an unshakable integrity that holds everything together. Though unease and desperation may linger quietly in the background, the spirit persistently calls us forward, urging us to evolve and rise above the illusions we face.

Even when anchored, our actions send ripples outward, shifting not only our personal reality but also the collective. In a world defined by motion and change, contentment remains elusive — until we align with the steady voice of our inner knowing.

Love your life

Our Art

Art, in every form, is a dialogue — with ourselves, with each other, and with the boundless. It mirrors who we are, what we feel, and how we interpret the world in any given moment. Through this ceaseless exchange, we delve into the depths of thought, emotion, and meaning that shape both our inner essence and the world around us.

. . .

Like me, my writing — my space for exploring the philosophical, spiritual, musical, and creative — is always evolving. I've been writing poetry, lyrics, music, reflective essays, and the occasional longer article for decades. But in 2015, I redesigned my approach and began a new chapter.

The inspiration for this piece originally came from Hugh Howey's article, "So You Want to Be a Writer." His advice, I believe, applies to almost any creative endeavor. Art, driven by passion or a sense of calling, demands more than fleeting interest. It requires periodic forays into all-out obsession and an unyielding commitment. Without this, we risk succumbing to distractions and shallow pleasures that leave our spirits hollow — endlessly chasing and searching for something unnamed.

Howey writes:

> *Practice. Everyone wants to write a novel, and they want to do it without stretching. You don't lace up and run a marathon without first learning to run a mile, two miles, five miles. The day you implement your plan is the day you start reading and the day you start writing. Start a blog and post to it every day. It might be a single line from a story that doesn't yet exist. Or a scene—maybe a first kiss or a bar fight. Maybe you write a different first kiss scene every day for a month. This is like practicing your layups. So when you have to nail one in a game, you*

don't freak out and go flying into the stands. The
importance of a blog is that your posts remain up
and visible forever ... the blog is your hub. This is
your street corner. This is where you strum your
instrument and improve.

Similarly, I enjoy walking or hiking daily. It's a way to experience life at a slower, more intentional pace. My mind often drifts into daydreams, even while listening to an audiobook, workshop, or interview. You may agree that the most profound insights, intuitions, and revelations often arise unexpectedly. These moments might feel like a simple *a-ha!* or hit like a wave of energy stopping you in your tracks, signaling that you've tapped into something significant. Either way, I trust they happen for a reason.

The challenge lies in pausing the endless stream of inputs and allowing our thoughts the freedom to flow without external triggers. Silence — uninterrupted and intentional — offers the space to process, integrate, and examine our perspectives. In this stillness, we actively listen and, in turn, learn more about ourselves.

Our art deserves the same focus and discipline. Engaging in the work sharpens our skills, stabilizes neural pathways, and allows us to meet inspiration with clarity when it arises. With repeated practice and every failure, the inner resistance and self-imposed barriers lose their power.

Howey also writes:

Find your voice ... it's the hardest, will take the
longest, but may be the most important thing you
ever do as a writer. What the hell is your voice? It's
how you write when you aren't aware that you're
writing. Everything else you do is mimicry. Self-
awareness is the enemy of voice. When you fire off
an email to your mom or best friend, you are
writing in your voice ... Your voice will change the
more you read and the more you write. That's
normal. It's still your voice.

Over the past thirty years, I've been discovering and refining my voice, expanding the scope of my writing along the way. I hope to continue honing it for the rest of my life. *Temet nosce* — know thyself.

Craft your learning, and learn your craft. The time we devote to creating is sacred. Surround yourself with those who inspire, challenge, and affirm your love for the journey. Be patient with yourself, but don't treat every step as precious. You cannot shape the sword without hammer, fire, and forge.

Creation unfolds naturally as we walk through life. *Solvitur ambulando* — it is solved by walking. Our stories are ever-evolving, as expansive as a deep breath: inhale and exhale; ebb and flow. Live in the moment, then let it go.

Never stop expressing and creating your art.

Love your life

THE HEART OF CHANGE

Change is a constant invitation. It challenges us to question, to grow, and to align with the deeper truths within ourselves, reshaping not only our lives but the pathways of thought and feeling that guide us.

. . .

We are always capable of making fundamental changes within ourselves, whether sudden or gradual. The mechanics of change lie in the brain. Our neural pathways form and solidify based on the activities we engage in most frequently. Just as beliefs are thoughts we repeatedly think, habits become ingrained in our bodies, and life responds accordingly. The world around us — this fantastic construct — reacts in the same way, regardless of how we wish it to be otherwise.

This explains why changing directions in life can feel so challenging. Awareness may reveal limiting or outdated patterns, opening up new possibilities. Yet, the greater challenge lies in follow-through. Once we choose a new path, perseverance is essential, especially in the early stages when results remain uncertain or unseen. However, we are rarely aware of the many gradual shifts happening within us or the subtle changes unfolding in the world around us.

Old pathways are stubborn — safe, familiar, and deeply entrenched, they resist change. Reinforced by years of energy flowing through them, they are not easily disrupted. It's natural to fear change, to doubt ourselves, or to project resistance onto those we perceive as obstacles. Resistance is part of the journey and should be expected.

Our internal chemistry — influenced by what we eat, where we live, and how we feel — also plays a role. Much of our default wiring was shaped in childhood, through experiences with parents, peers, books, play, and traumatic events. These early influences leave lasting impressions but don't have to define us forever.

We must also remember that core strengths lie outside the physical matrix. Even well-established neural pathways are responsive to new thoughts, imaginings, meditations, and intentions.

The heart is our other brain. Its intelligence is intuitive, holistic, and deeply connected to who we truly are. Unlike the brain's linear focus, the heart doesn't calculate; it perceives. It doesn't react; it responds. It bridges the seen and unseen, aligning us with authenticity and truth. The heart's neural network processes information, senses, and communicates. Beyond the science, it is where we feel profound experiences — love, grief, joy, fear — a visceral reminder of its central role in our lives.

Synchronizing the brain and heart unlocks extraordinary potential, harmonizing thought and feeling into clarity and insight. When we tune in to the heart's subtle wisdom, the path forward often becomes clear. This alignment makes reshaping old patterns not just possible, but inevitable.

Awareness is essential. Vibration is elemental. We live in an electric universe, where consciousness pulses with infinite potential, constantly building and awaiting expression. This creativity surrounds us, ready to be tapped into at any moment.

The greatest transformation comes not from the force of will alone, but from surrendering to these unseen forces — those that guide us toward our truest selves. When we listen to the wisdom of the heart, everything we seek will begin to unfold.

Mutatio est vocatio

Burn it Down: The Purifying Flame

Uncovering our deepest truth requires unraveling and unlearning the lies and limitations imposed by socialization, allowing us to burn away old burdens, making space for our true selves to return home.

. . .

When we strive to uncover our deepest, most authentic truth, we embark on a journey of unraveling and unlearning — freeing our spirits from the weight of conditioning. The lies, limits, and soul-stifling ideas imposed by socialization fall away as we let go.

Imagine a purifying flame, a powerful tool to allow whatever arises to emerge and simply burn away. Use your imagination. No hard feelings. No resentment. No disempowering guilt, self-deprecation, or self-reproach. Instead, fuel this fire with gratitude and love.

Thank you. You've served me well. Now, you may go.

Be grateful when old burdens resurface. The more familiar they feel, the more prepared you are to ignite them and let them burn. You no longer need them, and there's no reason to hold on. Trust that if something feels terrible, it's rooted in a lie. If it feels depressing, it's based on a lie. If it makes you feel degraded, deflated, uneasy, embarrassed, or disheartened — it's a lie.

These old ideas are bridges to places you've visited before. This time, you may be ready to burn them down. When you do, your heart will soften. Your mind will relax. Your clarity will be restored, and your true self will have the space to return home.

Solvitur ambulando

Inspired by *The Divine Arsonist: A Tale of Awakening,* by Jacob Nordby

CHANGE, OR DIE

*Change is not merely an event; it is the very fabric of life itself. In
every moment, we are offered the choice to evolve — to release the
old, embrace the new, and become more of who we are meant to be.*

. . .

Change is essential to life. Either we change, or we stagnate; we die.
It's unavoidable. If this truth causes stress or anxiety, it may stem
from the mistaken belief that anything in life is permanent.
Remember: you will "die" — so go ahead and get on with living.

We control our choices, actions, reactions, the information we
consume, and our perspective. But resisting change or clinging to
permanence only invites stress and stifles growth. Embracing
change and allowing ourselves to adapt is the key to healing,
fulfillment, and living authentically.

> *You taste it all: laughter and tears, bliss and
> boredom, the slings and arrows of existence. What
> never changes?*
>
> *What never changes is the constancy of change. You
> can always depend on it. Change is absolutely
> trustworthy.*
>
> — Jeff Brown

Popular culture often tells us that happiness depends on specific
forms of success. Dr. John Demartini observes that much of our
distress stems from two fears: losing what we seek and
encountering what we wish to avoid. These fears reveal conditioned
beliefs that limit what's possible.

True power lies in releasing expectations and surrendering to the
process. This means accepting life as it comes, just as it is. It's not
about being passive or giving up; it's about maintaining clarity of
purpose while letting go of the illusion that we control how our

desires manifest. Our higher self — the greater essence of who we are — knows what makes our hearts sing. When we trust this innate wisdom, everything relevant to our journey unfolds in the best way for where we are now and for everyone else.

Resistance to change restricts flow. Distrusting life's dynamic, ever-changing nature is ultimately a distrust of ourselves — and by extension, the intentions of others. This distrust keeps us on guard, creating resistance that accumulates in the mind and body, impeding their natural processes of healing and renewal. But when we trust life implicitly, we adapt organically, allowing healing and transformation to flow freely.

This is a call to embrace vitality and the full spectrum of being: excitement, passion, meaning, purpose, tears, joy, laughter, rage, and, above all, love. None of these exist without a willingness to change.

Change, or die.

Mutatio est vita, resistentia mortis

EMBRACING FEARLESSNESS

Feelings of helplessness arise when we are overwhelmed by external forces. Yet, by reconnecting with our inner compass and embracing fearlessness, we can rise above systems of control and manipulation, trust our intuition, and create space for personal growth and transformation.

. . .

Feelings of helplessness can drain our energy, leaving us overwhelmed by anxiety and stress. We often retreat into our own reality bubbles for self-preservation, locking ourselves in and keeping our hands firmly on the lock.

Until we reclaim our scattered focus from the overwhelming distractions of the outside world — things that seem important, powerful, and beyond our control — and reconnect with the eternal within, we remain disconnected from our inner compass. This disconnection makes us vulnerable to the agendas of those who thrive on control or seek to dominate others because they feel out of control of themselves.

It is time for fearlessness.

A storm will inevitably come, challenging us to confront our assumptions, question our beliefs, and reassess what we've unconsciously accepted. Systems built on control, manipulation, greed, and ignorance are doomed to fail. But we are adaptive, dynamic beings, inherently inclined toward the positive, even though our world often leans into the negative.

Accept the world as it is, not as you feel entitled to it, nor through the lens of misplaced ideals. With a firm grasp on reality and a clear comprehension of where you stand, no matter how long it takes — or how many lifetimes pass — we will always rise above those who seek to operate from lower, even parasitic, vibratory motives. Always.

It is time for fearlessness.

Embrace your intuitions and impulses, especially when they surprise you. Use this awareness to refine your discernment. Many of the old beliefs and patterns you've relied on for most of your life will no longer be compatible. Be prepared to let them go. Doing so will free up valuable space for new, more spiritually aligned desires and life-changing experiences.

You are a sovereign, infinite being.

It is time for fearlessness, for you have nothing to fear.

Love your life

WHATEVER ARISES

As we embrace our authentic selves and navigate the discomfort of uncertainty, we learn to love whatever arises — flaws, fears, and old patterns alike. This practice reclaims our power and creates space for growth, insight, and possibilities aligned with who we are now.

. . .

Delving into authenticity often stirs old issues, worries, and patterns to the surface. Our task is to transcend reflexive habits and grow comfortable with uncertainty. Attempts to control thoughts, feelings, or perceived flaws only tether us to past versions of ourselves. To move forward, we must choose acceptance, curiosity, and openness instead.

Loving whatever arises is neither defeat nor passivity. It is an act of reclamation and restoration, freeing us from mental constructs tied to outdated beliefs. This approach fosters recapitulation, or spiritual integration, clarity, and resonance with what is true now.

When the urge to deflect, blame, justify, or self-criticize emerges, resist the pull of distraction. Don't mask discomfort with entertainment, busyness, food, drink, or substances. Sit with it. Observe your separation from the thought or feeling — it is not you. It is a fabrication, a teaching tool, and it is transient. You, as the master of your journey, chose to experience and learn from it.

Every step of your path — from failure to triumph — has shaped you. Rising above old paradigms reveals the unique gift of who you are, a gift to the human collective. The limitless abundance of your heart offers fresh insight, intuition, and inspired direction for your next steps, aligned with your present self.

So, whatever arises, love that.

Love your life

TRUE TRANSFORMATION

True transformation comes not from fleeting external validation but from reconnecting with our authentic selves, rediscovering our core values, and embracing the deep, sustained passion that fuels meaningful change — a journey toward freedom that transcends superficial motivation.

. . .

In the Western world, we live enmeshed in a complex web of constraints, many of them subtle and disguised. By adulthood, most of us have abandoned our childhood dreams, settling into functional yet quietly desperate lives.

When defensiveness arises, its reasons and justifications become secondary. The urge to react is part of a deeper pattern, and breaking free from the paralysis and emotional strain it creates is essential.

Motivational speakers often exploit this sense of lack, fueling the manufactured fear of missing out. Their clever buzzwords, repetitive slogans, and even subtle hypnosis or mind control techniques may spark temporary excitement. However, we've outgrown the era of superficial motivation. Many have learned, through hard-earned experience, the limits of such fleeting inspiration.

Spending exorbitant amounts of money on workshops, seminars, and spiritual retreats often proves to be a waste of time and resources. While motivation can provide a nudge into action, true transformation demands a deeper, more intentional approach.

Motivation is formulaic, flashy, and focused on outcomes. Transformation, by contrast, is rooted in empathy, intentionality, and depth. The difference is critical, especially as modern change-makers, writers, teachers, and conscious activists lead from a place of genuine connection.

Motivation appeals to conformity, manipulation, and competition. Transformation, however, is built on curiosity, integration, collaboration, and self-discovery. It is an art: uncovering our values, strengths, and inherent gifts. Where motivation relies on shortcuts, transformation demands sustained passion — kindling, friction, and embers that burn with the white-hot heat of love.

Reconnecting with our dreams is a path to freedom. It allows us to rediscover the authentic, pristine source of our spirit's ambition — the true fountain of youth — and to live as our fullest selves: honest, whole, and complete.

We're in a time of profound transformation, both individually and collectively. True inspiration arises naturally when we stop forcing it. As the saying goes, we simply need to get out of our own way.

Solvitur ambulando

BACK TO THE TRUTH

Each of us finds our way back to the truth in our own time, guided not by external forces or manipulation but by the dynamic, ever-shifting circumstances we create for ourselves. The themes of our lives — struggles, successes, and everything in between — evolve as we grow and explore the deeper mysteries of existence. Truth reveals itself when we are ready.

· · ·

Everyone returns to the truth in their own time. No external influence, no matter how well-intentioned, can truly guide us home. If truth doesn't come from within, it remains borrowed, unreliable, and incapable of serving us in the long run.

We are masters of crafting circumstances that consistently attract the teachers, lessons, and growth opportunities we need — precisely when we need them. The universe operates dynamically, with potentialities constantly shifting, solidifying, and dissolving. The question is not *Why did I choose this reality?* but rather, *Which reality do I prefer?*

Our conscious minds do not operate at the level of shaping these dynamics; they were not designed to. These matters belong to the heart, the subconscious, and the superconscious — realms beyond linear and logical comprehension. Life unfolds frame by frame, yet in the space between every frame lies unseen magic. In that space resides our doorway through time.

The themes of this one short life become clear if we take the time to observe and accept: our world, our struggles, pains, challenges, victories, gifts, and natural talents. The stage, the set, and the players are always shifting because we are always changing. Yet, the story continues — integrating, challenging, validating, and demanding courage and authenticity. It thrives on questions and curiosity.

This story defies the fleeting, superficial meanings we often assign to it. No equation, theory, or doctrine can quantify the source of all that is.

What remains is the truth. And each of us will find it when we're ready.

In the meantime, we explore.

Iter nostrum veritatem ducit

The Illusion of Scarcity

We often let life play us by conforming to societal pressures, chasing external success, and accepting conditional relationships — all while operating from a belief in scarcity. True abundance, however, lies in shifting our perspective, embracing what is already present, recalibrating our inner compass, and releasing imposed expectations and outdated patterns.

. . .

We choose how, where, when, and with whom to engage in this game of life. The "what" and "why" are constants: we are here to learn — or perhaps, to remember. Yet, how often do we let the game play us?

Conditioned by our environment, we live in cultures steeped in a pervasive negative bias. Foundational archetypes and recurring themes surround us: struggle, polarity, and violence are glorified, while ease, grace, and lightness are dismissed as naive or insignificant. Fear of sickness, pain, and death is normalized, while joy in living, breathing, and experiencing spiritual freedom is seen as radical.

Misinformation, disinformation, capitalism, and divisive mainstream narratives keep us in a state of perpetual unease — or worse, trapped in chronic fight-or-flight. The more we conform to societal norms and political correctness, the less freedom our spirits have to explore and express their boundlessness.

In careers, we chase success, yet it's never enough. We seek money, accolades, or material gains to justify the pain and quiet desperation we endure, delaying necessary reality checks and existential soul-searching.

In relationships, we often settle for conditionality — chasing love, tolerating mediocrity, or trying to "fix" one another. We avoid asking value-based questions before committing and instead surrender to impulse, attraction, or infatuation — hoping, perhaps, that these critical issues will resolve themselves along the way. Worse, we may fixate on "red flags" or trivial concerns, sabotaging potentially meaningful connections, even if they are only to be short-lived. Beneath this lies an unconscious belief that we're unworthy of happiness, fulfillment, or stability. We rush toward connection while simultaneously pulling back, afraid of what it might mean to truly ask for and receive what we need.

As artists, we may be misled by distorted capitalist ideals, disappointed by a modest following, when in truth, a relatively small, engaged audience can sustain us throughout our entire career.

These spiritual checks and balances arise to gauge our commitment to purpose, inviting us to recalibrate our inner compass. Or perhaps the unsettling emotions point to lingering patterns protesting from beneath the surface. It may be time to sit quietly with these feelings, letting them sing their final verse before turning the page.

Scarcity thrives on lack — needing, wanting, seeking, and fearing we're missing out — concerns that are both unnatural and often externally imposed. Abundance, by contrast, is the knowing, remembering, and embodying of what is always present, beyond imposed expectations and conditions.

There is no lack of abundance. And yet, there persists a belief in an abundance of lack. Perspective is everything, and in the blink of an eye, we can shift the parameters of our reality.

Love your life

The Gift of Unfulfilled Desire

Unfulfilled passion — whether in romance, life, or personal aspirations — can be both painful and transformative, pointing us toward growth, resilience, and the search for deeper meaning. Struggle and dissatisfaction act as catalysts for renewal and the rekindling of our intrinsic drive for life.

. . .

Many of us have felt — or are currently feeling — the pangs of unfulfilled passion, whether it's a yearning for life itself, a partner, or an elusive dream.

Passion is the driving force of our lives. Those who dive deep, grab the rope, and pull themselves to the surface to ride the waves experience life in its fullest vibrancy. Others — perhaps the majority — dabble, suppress, or ignore this force, keeping busy in the shallow waters of distraction to avoid the discomforts of trying, failing, and trying again.

Yet stumbling is an essential part of pursuing and defining our passion, isn't it? Struggle sharpens our values, strengthens our resilience, and prepares us to navigate the challenges of this realm.

Beneath the physical facade of life lies an eternal fire. All things are energetic constructs bound by timeless consciousness. Stagnation is an illusion in a universe defined by perpetual change. Attempts to suppress, stifle, or compress life's flow only lead to friction, manifesting as discomfort or unexpected challenges. These remind us that life demands movement and expansion — it is, by nature, change.

In a constantly evolving world, we sometimes lose our connection to meaning and purpose, especially as material pursuits lose their luster. We instinctively create or attract events and circumstances to reawaken our passion and break through feelings of discontent.

However, drama often becomes a convenient but self-inflicted distraction from deeper issues we hesitate to confront. When disappointment, disillusionment, or resentment arise, the fire within dims, and parts of us withdraw into shadow. If left unchecked, we risk playing the victim to our own design.

Desperation often manifests subtly, through wanting or needing. When habitual, it spirals into self-sabotage. Yet it doesn't have to be this way. While our brains are wired to focus on the negative as a survival mechanism, deliberate effort to shift our attention to the positive yields deeper satisfaction and greater rewards over time.

Feeling unfulfilled is, in fact, a gift. It's a barometer, signaling that something vital is missing or being ignored. This feeling invites us to transmute discontent into creative, generative power — to rekindle the eternal flame and rediscover our genuine passion for life.

By embracing gratitude, we can reframe this sense of lack — often rooted in imperfect memories or past experiences — as a fleeting indicator. Observing it with detachment and curiosity allows us to extract the wisdom from each moment, burning away illusions and renewing our purpose with clarity and grace.

Love your life

ENTITLEMENT

Entitlement, driven by a scarcity mindset, has become deeply ingrained in modern society, fostering narcissism, materialism, and a relentless pursuit of external validation. This mindset traps us in cycles of dissatisfaction and disconnection. True fulfillment lies not in material possessions or societal expectations but in embracing vulnerability, personal growth, and the richness of authentic life experiences.

. . .

Entitlement is a pervasive force in our culture. Many aspects of modern life have devolved into narcissism, moral relativism, and sensationalized drama — trends rooted in certain academic and social movements. This mindset is further amplified by vocal minorities, "woke" mobs, PR firms, and ideologues driving cancel culture, all dominating public discourse.

At its core, entitlement stems from a scarcity mindset that distorts our relationships, careers, and personal sense of worth. It pushes us into defensive, even aggressive, stances, blocking the patience, awareness, and heart-centered decision-making needed for meaningful connection. Left unchecked, entitlement drains us spiritually, leaving behind emptiness and apathy.

For many of us over the age of thirty, the mantra "Work hard, and you'll succeed" was deeply ingrained. Passed down from parents who lived in an era when jobs offered long-term stability and clear paths to success, this belief carries profound consequences. We sacrifice and strive, convinced that hard work entitles us to rewards — the car, the house, the respect, and the status. Yet as we achieve these markers of success, we often find ourselves wanting more: a bigger house, a better car, a flawless family, and external admiration.

This relentless pursuit leads to a crossroads: victimhood or martyrdom. Our lives become defined by rigid worldviews and the expectations of others, perpetuating cycles of competition and inadequacy. We rush through life, burdened by external pressures and the relentless ticking of time, while neglecting the present moment. The harder we try to control and manipulate our circumstances, the more this resistance manifests in our stressed bodies and restless minds.

Yet we are capable of so much more. The real "work" is not about achieving or "deserving" more but about embracing the truth of who we are. This truth, often obscured by the distractions of daily life, reveals that deep and profound meaning is found not in possessions but in experiences — in the moments of discovery, challenge, passion, and raw emotion that define authentic living.

If we are brave enough to embrace it, we are, in fact, entitled to a life of authenticity, trust, and vulnerability. There is no blueprint for this journey; it is not about certainty but about growth, exploration, and the courage to ask, "What if?" Life's true richness lies in the moments when we dare to step into the unknown.

You, like everyone else, are entitled to your uniqueness, your untapped potential, and the fullness of life's experiences.

Love your life

THE LONELY JOURNEY

The world is in constant motion, ever shifting and changing. While some retreat into quiet solitude to process the turbulent energies of change, others are swept up in the relentless pace of daily obligations and countless distractions. Yet, even in our most solitary moments, we are never truly alone. Each of us is navigating a personal revolution, confronting challenges that, though they may feel deeply personal, are threads woven into the collective human experience.

. . .

The world is undergoing profound change, though perhaps it always has been. In response, many of us increasingly seek solitude, intentionally isolating ourselves to integrate and understand the intense energies emerging within and around us. Others may avoid this inner reckoning, immersing themselves in busyness and the unrelenting demands of society's constructs.

Yet regardless of our approach, none of us is ever truly alone. Every individual, in their own way, is grappling with energetic, spiritual, and deeply personal upheaval.

For those striving to grow and heal, it's natural to wish that others would live with greater consciousness and passion. But choosing to embark on a journey of rapid spiritual healing can make us our own harshest critics. We may unconsciously project this inner turbulence onto others, compounding feelings of guilt, shame, and judgment. In these moments, we often retreat — not necessarily in physical isolation, but inwardly, where our imagination becomes a playground for shadow work.

It's important to remember: feelings of lack, unworthiness, guilt, shame, or pain may be overwhelming, but they are temporary. They can be triggered by seemingly insignificant events and overshadow an otherwise beautiful day. Yet, like the next heartbeat, they are fleeting. These emotions linger only until we accept the truths they point to within us.

The transience of something does not diminish its significance; meaning is ours to uncover. Neither vulnerability nor shame are signs of weakness. Though these emotions may manifest differently for men and women, their roots are nourished by the same falsehood — the belief that "I am not enough."

When we sit in stillness and allow what arises to be seen, we validate our experience. This quiet acknowledgment lets the energies unravel, releasing their hold over time and offering us their wisdom in return.

But healing doesn't require retreating to a cave or vanishing into the wilderness. As we clarify our values, we can use tools and practices that resonate with us, wherever we are. By listening to the quiet voice of intuition and instinct, we learn to communicate authentically — with ourselves and with others.

The struggle may feel cosmic and complex, but trust and love remain universal and profoundly simple. Through them, we reconnect to the richness of life and the shared humanity that binds us all.

Solvitur ambulando

Through the Veil of Artifice

We live in a world saturated with distractions and manipulated narratives that encourage us to fear and suppress our true selves. From consumerism and violence to societal expectations and psychological manipulation, we've been conditioned to conform and disconnect from our authentic power. To reclaim our purpose and inner truth, we must break free from these artifices, confront our fears, and reconnect with the divine essence within us.

. . .

How much do we truly fear being our authentic selves? Quite a bit, it seems. Fiction, fantasy, violence, and other superficial constructs dominate our cultural landscape, reinforcing the belief that life is about struggle, distrust, materialism, and conflict. These narratives disconnect us from our true essence.

We're told what to believe, how to act, and what to value. The lines are drawn, and we're afraid to color outside them. In seeking belonging, we lose sight of who we truly are, doubting our intuition and surrendering to a hive mindset that replaces personal purpose with collective conformity.

But it doesn't have to be this way.

At any moment, we can change course. The systems that perpetuate fear, consumerism, and shame are sustained only by our continued compliance and complicity. These constructs exist to keep us distracted and disconnected. To reclaim our authenticity, we must recognize the invisible strings of societal programming and remember: we were created to be magnificent. You are divine! The forces controlling the narrative profit from your confusion and disillusionment, shaping false values to maintain power.

The truth is simple: nothing holds inherent meaning until we assign it. Every belief and attachment must be questioned — "Whose idea is this?" and "Is it even true?" Unless we remain awake and aware, our energy will serve someone else's agenda. Those in power thrive on consuming your creativity and potential.

Return to the source. True meaning resides within you.

Reignite the purifying flame of your truth. This flame clears your vision, restores your heart, and reveals what no longer serves you. It breaks apathy, disrupts the numbness that keeps you from living fully, and reignites your innocence, resilience, and spiritual resonance. Yes, it will scare you — growth often does. But it will also deepen your empathy and reconnect you with what is real.

Your truth is profound, invigorating, and light. You'll feel it when you let go of the distractions. It is undeniable and will guide you through fear, which is merely a passing storm on the way to greater understanding.

The only thing standing between you and your fullest potential is the fear of who you truly are. So, dive in.

Temet nosce

Passion or Anger?

Outside influences will always challenge our inner compass, and the noise of outdated ideas can irritate or even inflame the creative spirit. In these moments, we face a pivotal choice: to act from passion or anger.

Both are powerful motivators, capable of driving us to action, but the difference lies in the energy we choose to project into the world and the values that guide us.

Anger embodies resistance — fear, dissonance, vengeance, control, revolt, and violence.

Passion embodies surrender — love, purpose, ingenuity, independence, freedom, and creation.

Awareness is key. Mindfulness of who we are, what we are doing, and why we are doing it shapes the outcomes we manifest.

The journey itself is the reward — an endless road of discovery and growth. What we create holds the power to heal or harm, to inspire or inflame.

Choose your energy wisely.

Ira resistit, passio creat

ARISE FROM THE ASHES:
ON HEALING AND RENEWAL

Within us, a quiet war rages — a battle between the stories we've inherited and the truths waiting to be discovered. But just as life renews itself after a forest fire, healing emerges from the ashes of shame and self-doubt. In every place we feel broken lies a seed of resilience, ready to grow into something stronger and more authentic.

. . .

I used to believe I would never be worthy of a truly worthy partner in life unless I "made something" of myself. Though I know where that belief came from, I'm still not entirely sure what it means. These philosophical weeds are something we all have in our gardens, aren't they? What I do know is that this narrative isn't just a story — it's a spiritual and emotional prison, a self-imposed penance for an imagined crime. While it takes time for the scars of shame to fade, I'm grateful that awareness has sparked a slow but cumulative process of healing.

When we live by these egoistic, self-proclaimed mission statements, we lose sight of the bigger picture. Measures of success or worthiness are entirely subjective, endlessly ambiguous. We move our own goalposts repeatedly, striving toward an ideal that can never truly be met. This internal dissonance creates tremendous strain, manifesting as cycles of depression, apathy, indecisiveness, frustration, and anxiety. This pressure seeps into our daily lives, hidden beneath layers of responsibilities, obligations, and distractions. We avoid the pain unconsciously and wonder why the uneasiness persists. Sooner or later, we must confront the discontinuity and deception we've created within ourselves.

> *I am convinced that the jealous, the angry, the bitter, and the egotistical are the first to race to the top of mountains. A confident person enjoys the journey, the people they meet along the way, and sees life not as a competition. They reach the summit last*

*because they know God isn't at the top waiting for
them. He is down below, helping his followers to
understand that the view is glorious wherever you
stand.*

— Shannon Alder

We live in a culture that glorifies heroes, champions, and those who
make great sacrifices. Yet, paradoxically, it also fixates on villains,
narcissists, and the violently notorious. Ironically, we often turn on
the very heroes we once admired, as envy and resentment bubble to
the surface. This cultural polarization seeps into our subconscious,
leaving fertile ground for the seeds of guilt, shame, and self-
reproach to take root.

When we embark on the perilous journey back to our center, our
intrinsic truth casts a blinding light on everything we've tried to
conceal. Guilt and shame amplify our vulnerabilities, shaking us to
our core. Yet this unraveling is necessary. It's through this
reckoning that we reconnect with the original source — the still,
small voice buried beneath the layers of programming and
conditioning imposed by our earthbound lives.

If we're in a relationship during this period of spiritual revolution,
the energy of transformation spares no one. This force operates
outside the bounds of time and convenience. Sometimes, we're
fortunate to share this path with someone undergoing their own
process of awakening. Though they may be just as terrified as we
are, their knowing smile can be both wicked and reassuring. These
blessed synchronicities are gifts to those brave enough to confront
the flames. Two hearts aligned in this way intensify the fire,
accelerating purification and transformation.

This journey may lead to a deeper, more meaningful partnership or
the renewal of one. If so, the bond will exist on a higher vibration
— more authentic, attuned, and pure than anything that could have
existed before. Yet we must trust in the natural timing of life,
knowing that our strongest desires do not always dictate our lived
experiences.

Too often, when we look at fire, we see only destruction. To me, fire has always been a natural, unapologetic force of renewal — a recycling of energies, a structural reformation. In our clumsy attempts to control it, we forget that its purpose is transformation, not annihilation. In nature, after a forest fire passes, flora and fauna immediately respond, embracing the newness with an innate resolve and a knowing beyond words.

Life is neither static nor stagnant. It is forever done and undone, finished and unfinished. But the Light never fades.

> *All that is gold does not glitter,*
> *Not all those who wander are lost;*
> *The old that is strong does not wither,*
> *Deep roots are not reached by the frost.*
>
> *From the ashes a fire shall be woken,*
> *A light from the shadows shall spring;*
> *Renewed shall be blade that was broken,*
> *The crownless again shall be king.*

— J.R.R. Tolkien, *The Fellowship of the Ring*

Ex tenebris, lux redit

THE SELF WE SACRIFICE: ON CONFORMITY

External pressures often influence our choices, making it easy to lose sight of who we truly are. A lack of self-awareness leads to conformity, while embracing our authentic selves is essential for living a meaningful and fulfilling life.

. . .

There's a saying: *If you don't stand for something, you'll fall for anything.*

Many of us recognize the truth of this, even as we pretend to be unaffected by it — especially in our relationships. But the most debilitating relationship we face is often the one we have with ourselves. Consider these variations of the saying:

- If you don't stand up for yourself, you'll defer to anyone, regardless of their quality or character.

- If you don't know who you are, you'll be told who to be.

- If you don't stand for something, you stand for nothing; you're merely a sheep.

- If you don't have confidence, you'll be intimidated by strength, whether real or imagined.

- If you don't make a commitment, you'll waffle in perpetual indecision.

- If you don't have a purpose in life, you'll never find meaning — you'll live by someone else's design.

Many people live by these unspoken, socially accepted directives. As we can see, there's a lot at stake — energetically, spiritually, mentally, and even physically. How often do we use strategies and compromises to fit in or feel good? How often do we settle for less than the ideal just to feel wanted? How often do we sell out for rewards, favors, or profit? How often do we rely on the passionate words of others instead of listening to the truth that rests forever within our hearts? How often do we wear masks, speaking pleasantries to appear polite, politically correct, socially accepted, or commercially successful?

There is a pervasive superficiality in our culture that leaves a bitter taste in the soul. It provokes corrosive, self-defeating behaviors like deflecting, projecting, shaming, and gossiping. To cope with our perceived insignificance and insecurity, we often hide behind these limiting social facades.

Sadly, these postures rob us of joy and drain our vitality, keeping us hovering somewhere between normal and numb. If that isn't good enough for you, it might be time to reconsider your motivations — but resist the urge to engage in self-reproach or judgment.

Live, listen, and learn:

- We compromise too much to belong.

- We suppress too much to feel safe.

- We defend too much to be vulnerable.

We forget that living from our true selves is what defines, attracts, and manifests the things that resonate with us most authentically.

In other words, our reality reflects who we truly are — not who we wish to be or pretend to be.

Every moment, in every circumstance, offers a new opportunity to make a better, more aligned, and simpler choice — though it's rarely the easiest.

Nobody wants to be lonely, but no one is ever truly alone. Close your eyes and breathe into your heart. You'll remember that you are safe. You are this — and so much more.

You are enough.
You are important.
You are essential to this earthly dance.
You are an entirely original song, as beautiful as the wind and as playful as time.

You... be you.

Veritas tua te liberabit

Healing the Inner Rift

In a world driven by money, societal expectations, and fear, we often lose connection with our true selves. To live authentically, we must release outdated beliefs, trust our inner wisdom, and shift from passive desire to active creation — embracing love, vulnerability, and self-worth as our birthright.

. . .

Money, a construct around which our civilization revolves, epitomizes our act of assigning value, influence, and power to fleeting thoughts, feelings, and objects. It holds meaning only because we collectively agree it does, enabling its manipulation by those in power. Similarly, pain, polarity, and societal divisions gain value through our fear, longing, and attempts to belong. These forces have shaped a world defined by imbalance, now being challenged by an era of reckoning and rebalancing.

The chaos of this transition may feel overwhelming, but lightness requires no effort. It calls us to return to center — our natural state — by releasing the illusions that bind us to negativity. Much of what we carry, from inherited beliefs to emotional wounds, must be reconciled with new understandings.

This shift also transforms relationships, infusing them with higher vibrations and a more evolved understanding of love, equality, and partnership. Yet residual fears and outdated ideas cloud our intuition, perpetuating loneliness even in the presence of others. We cling to old patterns of wanting and needing instead of embracing the joy of having and being.

To move forward, we must release shame, guilt, and resentment — burdens passed down through generations. These emotional scars, along with unconscious coping mechanisms, have shaped our mistrust of vulnerability and fear of happiness. But in this age of heightened awareness, we bear the responsibility to process, integrate, and let go of these shadows, reclaiming our power and self-trust.

We are capable of amazing things. To be our truest selves, we must recognize that we deserve love — deeply, passionately, and unconditionally. There is no question of our belonging or purpose here.

Our hearts carry a musical truth, resonant with a love divine. It is what we truly are.

Love your life

P.S. What if this is the life you've always wanted? What if you're doing just fine? What if it's all going to work out? What if you are loved, just for being you? What if you are divine, infinite, unshakable, safe, and supernatural? What if there really is nothing to fear? Every breath is a lifetime. Every thought a new reality. Listen to the realness that occasionally hides beneath the banal, inane lies of this matrix. Heed your true impulse. Walk on.

UNRELIABLE IDENTITY

Our identities shape our choices and actions, often trapping us in familiar but limiting patterns. As old beliefs unravel, we are called to simplify and embrace authenticity, recognizing that wholeness and fulfillment lie beyond the transient and controllable aspects of life.

. . .

What we identify with shapes our reality. Every decision we make is influenced by our experiences, values, and cultural conditioning. Stepping into the unfamiliar can feel terrifying because it challenges our comfort zones and exposes us to the fear of losing control. This is our reality bubble: a self-contained world where we live, often disconnected from others, no matter how much we empathize with or relate to them.

As creators of our lives, resisting change keeps us tethered to familiar patterns. These well-worn identities — like old, comfortable clothes — offer a sense of safety but often perpetuate suffering. We journey onward, uncertain and unsettled, unable to escape ourselves. To cope, we craft carefully curated presentations: versions of ourselves that meet social expectations while concealing deeper truths.

In time, upheaval becomes inevitable. Competing thoughts, emotions, and motivations can leave us stuck in survival mode, drained by the effort to maintain control. But perhaps it's time to examine the attachments that hold us back. Life calls us to simplify, for living authentically demands that we let go of what no longer serves us and embrace what feels, and is, real.

Wholeness and fulfillment aren't found in clinging to old identities. By shedding the layers we've outgrown, we create space for the truth of who we are to emerge — free, unburdened, and fully alive.

Vero nihil veri

BOOKMARKS

Life unfolds in unexpected ways when we release the need for control and trust the flow. By recognizing that everything is interconnected, we discover that the power to shape our reality lies in being present, mindful, and aware of the choices we make in each moment.

. . .

We never know when something — or someone — will open the door to a new chapter or beginning. This is the limitation of linear thinking: we plan, anticipate, and try to control. We push, demand, and insist. Yet grace and ease emerge when we trust the flow — when we follow omens, honor intuitive impulses, believe in unexpected blessings, and feel our way through life.

The struggle often lies in the noise of the day-to-day: alarms, schedules, jobs, careers, and endless obligations that pull us away from any freedom for our thoughts, or pursuing our joy. Drained of energetic resources, we focus only on what's directly in front of us, forgetting that what lies just beyond our awareness might offer the shift in perspective we need most.

Everything is interconnected. Life flows effortlessly beyond the mental constructs and limitations we impose. Too often, we overlook seemingly insignificant moments, only to realize later how essential they were to the story.

Reflecting on our journey, we begin to see how choices, intentions, and creative energy weave the tapestry of our lives. In these moments of recognition, we remember the quiet yet profound power we hold to shape what comes next.

Life is a book we write in real time, each moment a new sentence, each choice a bookmark, each turning point a fresh chapter. The beauty of this story lies not only in its unexpected twists but in our conscious engagement with it. Curiosity is a superpower.

The past shapes us, the future remains unwritten, and the present is where it all unfolds. While the experiences we choose to explore during our lifetime define parts of our narrative, the meaning we give them, the way we carry them forward, and the stories we tell are decisions that rest entirely in our hands and hearts.

There are no ordinary moments — only pages waiting to be written.

Love your life

THE LIVING STORY

Life is like editing a film: we selectively highlight key moments, filter experiences, and shape our story based on who we are and who we interact with. Yet the depth and authenticity of our narrative come from embracing every part of our journey — including the struggles — and recognizing that everything, from our choices to our emotions and experiences, matters in crafting a meaningful and true life story.

. . .

In my experience as a film and video editor, one of the most common challenges is having enough raw content to create something meaningful, cohesive, and impactful. So much is decided in fractions of a second — often by just a few frames — and we can quickly run out of usable material. Editing is, after all, a form of manipulation; it shapes pacing, meaning, theme, structure, and even perception.

Similarly, as we journey through life, we consciously and unconsciously edit our own stories, highlighting key memories, defining moments, and emotional milestones. This ongoing process evolves as we grow, learn, unlearn, stumble, fall, and rise again.

Every now and then, particularly in new relationships or when faced with the classic "tell me about yourself" prompt, our internal story editor springs into action. To convey the essence of our lives, we filter a vast library of experiences, presenting events selectively based on who we are in that moment and the audience before us.

Some embellish the details, acting as marketers of their own lives. Others swing to the opposite extreme, downplaying their achievements out of modesty, fear, guilt, or shame. Without reflecting on or rehearsing how we tell our story, we may struggle to connect the dots, presenting an incomplete or disjointed version of ourselves.

But there's always more beneath the surface. Whether you're 20, 40, or 60 years old, you've lived anywhere from 7,300 to 22,000 days — surely that's enough material to create a rich, meaningful narrative, right?

Like the most remarkable sculptures, which emerge only after countless chisels and chips, the essence of our life story is revealed through the accumulation of thoughts, decisions, and experiences along the way.

We shouldn't dismiss the depth of our story to avoid embarrassment, appease others, or conceal our pain. Everyone experiences the same spectrum of emotions — fear, love, worry, trust, anger, anxiety, and ease. These universal human conditions connect us all.

Yet, our culture leans heavily toward "saving face," sometimes to the point of altering appearances with surgery, cosmetics, or digital filters. We say one thing while omitting another, risking the erosion of our true selves. Life can easily become a thin, superficial fiction — a "based on a true story" narrative shaped by external pressures and media distortions, where the truth is often lost.

Courage is the root of authenticity. Authenticity lays the foundation for vulnerability. Vulnerability invites surrender, allowing us to integrate the fragmented parts of our being and complete the puzzle of who we truly are.

The depth of our character lies in the understanding that everything matters: every experience, every choice, and every person who crosses our path. Each moment adds to the richness of our unique and meaningful story.

Love your life

OWNING THE STORY

We carry the echoes of those who came before us — their struggles, joys, and unfinished stories — woven into the fabric of our own, shaping who we are until we choose to awaken, unravel, and reweave the threads with intention and grace.

. . .

My parents were never able to provide the emotional support or conscious partnership each needed from the other. They valued different things and spoke in different love languages. In my view, they were never able to express these unmet needs. They had children, so they pushed through and made it work as best they could. They came from a different generation and culture — one shaped by struggle, endurance, perseverance, self-sacrifice, and, unfortunately, a quiet, deep-seated desperation.

It took me years to piece together the fragments of turmoil I had unconsciously internalized. I carried these burdens as truth — until I didn't. There was blame, until there wasn't. There was guilt, now gone. There was shame, and now, far less. Eventually, we all reach a point of balance — our spiritual and existential center.

When my parents separated, I began to see them differently — as individuals, rather than roles. It was a revelation. I finally understood some of their childhood struggles and connected the dots in their stories. This insight illuminated their personal — and relational — difficulties. Every so often, another small piece of their past emerges through casual conversation. They may have lacked the tools we have today and, perhaps more importantly, the capacity to hold space for each other. These are not excuses but reasons for empathy. Live, learn, and listen.

Our reality demands that we take responsibility for our own story. It's the only way to move beyond the noise and uncover the ease, grace, and joy that lie beneath the surface. This is awareness. This is conscious sensitivity. It's about liberating our hearts and opening our eyes.

Each of us is like a needle — the stylus on the vinyl record of life. This divine design transmits our music into the world. There will be scratches, skips, repetitions, and fleeting atonal distortions, but the song always continues. It is empowering to realize that nothing lasts forever and that what we carry from this journey are the vibrations of our unique music.

Owning your story means acknowledging and accepting what was, taking full responsibility for who you are now, and aspiring to heal, adapt, and grow. Fueling this process with awareness and gratitude amplifies the vibrancy, vividness, and volume of your life's song. To embrace gratitude is to honor all those who helped shape it.

Temet nosce

TAPPING THE SOURCE

Source energy — whether we call it nature, the Universe, or something else — is the ethereal energy we tap into daily, shaping our reality through our thoughts, choices, and perceptions. By connecting with this energy and aligning with our deeper truth, we can live with greater consciousness, empowerment, and trust in the flow of life.

. . .

When we think of "the source," we might associate it with nature, metaphysics, the teachings of Abraham-Hicks, or the vastness of the Universe — concepts that, for some, may carry a vague "woo-woo" connotation and lack grounded meaning. For others, it may simply serve as another way of expressing a belief in the unseen or divine. Yet, regardless of the label we choose, the essence remains the same: an all-pervasive energy or field that we continuously access, consciously or unconsciously, in every moment of our lives. Beyond the rituals, labels, or practices we adopt, what truly matters is discovering what resonates deeply enough to connect us to the heart of all things.

Most of us live far below our true potential. We move through life on autopilot, colliding with each other, bound by outdated limitations, and rarely engaging with anything beyond what our physical senses dictate. This unconscious, disconnected state traps us in cycles of drama and chaos, leaving us blind to the greater forces at work.

We often see ourselves as passive victims of reality — at the mercy of external forces, convinced our minds are too small to comprehend the bigger picture. In this mindset, we forget a vital truth: we are the creators of our lives.

But what if we paused for a moment to step outside the old narrative?

What if everything in our lives right now is a reflection of the choices, thoughts, and actions we've made thus far? What if some of it carries over from past lives — or even reaches ahead from future ones? What if the thread of our experience stretches far beyond this single lifetime, weaving into a larger, interconnected tapestry?

The truth is, source energy is always at work, especially in the present moment. What we see, feel, taste, touch, and perceive is filtered through the lens of our unique perspective and shaped by the evolving interpretations we bring to the world.

Our bodies are transient temples for our souls and, in the grander sense, constructs of our spirit — triune representations designed to explore the eternal while temporarily rooted in the physical. Emotions, feelings, and intuitions are tools meant to guide and empower us, helping us align with our deepest truth: that we are safe, eternal, and loved.

This is the essence of embodied consciousness. Our thoughts, intentions, and awareness shape the world around us. When we surrender to this flow, trust the process, and remain present, we sync with the natural rhythm of life — a rhythm in which everything unfolds as it should, offering exactly what we need in each moment.

Solvitur ambulando

TIME THIEF: ON COMPLAINING

Energy is our most precious resource, yet we lose it in countless ways — through distractions, negative patterns, and unconscious choices. In a world where time feels fleeting and external forces profit from our disengagement, reclaiming our power begins with awareness. And one of the most subtle yet pervasive drains on that energy is the habit of complaining.

. . .

In this linear world, we lose, give away, or have our energy stolen in countless ways — energetically, psychically, physically, and temporally. Each day, we consciously choose how to spend our limited moments, minutes, hours, and years, exploring life and allowing it to unfold. Yet, when we live unconsciously, disconnected from the present, time slips through our fingers. Meanwhile, those who are aware and pulling the strings profit from our squandered talents and unrealized potential.

One of the most subtle and insidious ways we waste energy is through complaining. While it's easy to find endless things to gripe about, most complaints are superficial distractions or manufactured grievances. Internalizing them — whining, railing against circumstances, or blaming others — poisons the spirit and siphons away resources that could be better spent elsewhere.

Look around. You'll see it in your own reflection, in the routines of unfulfilled friends and family, and in the weary faces of strangers. It's palpable in classrooms and boardrooms, woven into tired societal narratives, and evident in the processed food we consume. Complaining has become so habitual, so normalized, that it shapes our physical and mental states to accommodate it.

When we give in to this habit, we trap ourselves in limiting perceptions that keep us stuck. These perceptions might align with momentary frustrations, but they rarely lead to a fulfilling or meaningful life. Instead, we adapt to merely coping, tolerating, or enduring — all while suppressing our discontent until it inevitably reaches a boiling point.

But we shouldn't let it go that far. Our mental health, our wellbeing, and our potential for a fulfilling life are too valuable to sacrifice. True change begins in the present moment. It starts with becoming aware: listening to your inner voice, observing the inner critic, and resisting the external impulses to judge, blame, or react. Whether it's snapping at a tailgating driver or railing against the corporatocracy that owns and operates the world, pause and ask yourself: *Is this the story I want to live?*

Get real. Be honest. Tap into the original source within you. Remember who you are and what truly matters. These stories — these constructs of frustration and blame — might feel as tangible as a stubbed toe or a rolled ankle in the moment, but in the grand scheme, they are fleeting distractions.

Redirect your energy into what uplifts and empowers you. Invest in your courage and creativity, and follow the impulses of your soul. Choose the evolving, expansive paradigms that call you to live a life of possibility, passion, and purpose.

It's your story. So, what will be your legacy?

Love your life

TIME THIEF: ON WORRYING

Worry is a quiet thief, disguising itself as preparation while weighing us down with fear and control. It convinces us that by dwelling on what might happen, we're protecting ourselves from pain. To break free, we must understand its roots, challenge its illusions, and learn to trust in life's natural flow.

. . .

Why worry? Because of fear. Fear manifests in countless shades of gray — a numbing palette that dims a sunny day or deepens the gloom of an overcast sky. When fear takes the form of worry, it becomes especially tragic.

Worry is rooted in a sense of powerlessness and victimhood that can seep into our very core. It readily takes up residence in our hearts if we allow it. By worrying, we place our trust in our distrust of everything.

In our fear-driven culture, we worry about nearly everything: money, education, sex, health, politics, the environment, the planet, the unknown — whether it's from the skies above or beneath the surface of the Earth. We worry about conflicts, "viruses," chemtrails, waking, sleeping, living, dying, making a difference, our souls, our bodies, the afterlife, even what to do if we win the lottery.

But what is worry, really? It doesn't help us function well. We survive, yes, but merely surviving is a long way from thriving.

Worry is a symptom of our belief in the linear, controlled nature of life. It provides a false sense of grounding while ultimately paralyzing us. At its core, worry is about trying to control everything — our feelings, our outcomes, our experiences — because we fear the pain that might come from losing control or facing what we'd rather avoid.

We. Fear. Pain. Yet, we place far too much faith in its potential for misery, striving to control everything in an attempt to avoid it. The tragedy is this: the human spirit does not respect control. Not in the slightest. While pain is inevitable, suffering is optional.

We believe that if we don't control our thoughts, we'll lose our minds, our choices, or our peace. If we don't control our children, they'll spiral out of control. If we don't control our finances, we'll go bankrupt. If we don't control our relationships, they'll fall apart.

If we don't control the world around us — through endless wars, manipulative trade policies, or incessant propaganda — someone else might gain influence, and that is simply unacceptable.

Control, at best, is a harmful illusion. Fortunately, we can learn to mitigate its extremes. By raising our awareness and breaking outdated patterns, we can detach from the need to control and instead engage in the flow of life. But this process takes time — it won't happen overnight.

Worry, like all negative emotions, is a barometer. It signals that something needs our attention. *Where did this worry come from? Who does it belong to? What do I gain from holding on to it? Is it even real? Is it true?*

To worry less, we must shift our focus to trusting the natural flow and timing of life. Life is always happening, always in motion. It is immeasurable, unpredictable, and beautifully uncontainable. Life simply *is*.

Love your life

BOUNDLESS

Your heart is a powerful, instantaneous feedback mechanism, the core of deep feeling and your original source, always ready to challenge limiting beliefs and illusions.

Negative thoughts, repeated over time, can slowly shrink your life-affirming energy, which yearns to expand and ripple through the world, touching all the lives you encounter with your unique magnificence.

You are loved, no matter the illusions you hold, but always remember that lightness and freedom are just a breath away, waiting for you.

Love your life

Departures

Only when we authentically release the old ways can we truly move forward. By integrating the lessons, experiences, and essence presented to us, while dissolving our attachments, we create fertile ground for the seeds of our deepest desires to take root, flourish, and multiply.

Our realities inevitably align with what resonates most profoundly, as our minds and bodies instinctively return to what is remembered, conditioned, or ingrained, often without conscious awareness or deliberate focus.

Suffering and misery feel safe when they are the most familiar, and we excel at sabotaging our own energetic momentum, resisting the leap into the unknown. Yet, this is only one possibility.

Solvitur ambulando

RELENTLESS DICHOTOMY

This place is remarkably beautiful
And also remarkably sick
The way we exist
On the precipice
Astounds and amazes me

I, and many like me
Came back again
To tell it like it is
To shatter the bullshit
To trance-send the lies
To catalyze, initialize
To instigate, investigate
To expose the old ways
And challenge the cowards;

The weak of spine
And weak of mind;
Those of malice and
Manipulation;

Those who laugh, smile
Profit and wile
At the many who try
To play along
But know in their hearts
There is another way...

You can choose to be
A background player
To be safe, numb
And follow the obvious path
Until you're waiting
Desperately
Quietly
To die...

Or, you can listen

Shut up and listen

You can write your song

You can tell your story, and
Let it go where it wants to go

Where it needs to go

And just know
That in the end
It's all good

No Apologies

Do not apologize for what drives you. Don't be afraid of it, either.

Don't be afraid of expressing your pain or your love.

Explore the caves and caverns formed by the shadows, especially if you're shaking in your boots. As your light grows brighter while you descend, leave only the charred impressions of exploded illusions along the rocky walls for future explorers to interpret and decipher as they see fit.

A single frame of your life is worth a thousand words, and it undoubtedly demonstrates the power of the moment, but it completely disregards the billions of thoughts and moments that make up your story.

You are here right now. All of you. You're not done yet.

Memento vivere
Vive veritatem

TIRED

We are tired
Beaten, now and again, by our
Weighted struggles
Inside, outside,
Broadside

We are traveled
Seeking, now and again, for our
Ounce of solace
Inside, outside
Ringside

The discontent
Paid its rent
Well in advance, yet
Ours is the choice
To circumnavigate the universe,
Or to mire the vessel in the
Made-to-believe

Solvitur ambulando;
Walk
Discover
Recover
Resolve
Evolve
Love

DIVINE TIMING

We can't control the timing of outcomes. These calculations are beyond the mind, existing in the unrestricted, boundless dance of energy and light.

Our higher selves, however, are celebrating, for the spirit of our infinity knows what lies ahead.

In this space, our task is to trust the flow and allow the unraveling mystery to manifest in the most beneficial way for all.

We may experience suffering in the meantime as our minds replay well-practiced anxieties, scripts, beliefs, and expectations. Yet, countless hours spent exploring the depths of insecurity, paranoia, fear, and frustration are blessings — lessons and opportunities for greater lightness, healing, and trust in the love and freedom that lie beneath.

Love your life

The Practice of Presence

It may not always make sense to our linear programming, but it always works to our benefit. There is no such thing as wasted time or energy; it's all in our perception. And you can't fall behind in this life.

Choices drive momentum, and whether we're conscious of our movements or not, the pieces of our lives are constantly structuring the cosmos of our environment and stimulating our senses. If we're still waking up each morning — out of hyperdream and into the deliberate — we're still alive in this story. We're still relevant, still seeking, writing, exploring, learning, teaching, dancing, and demanding expansion and expression.

Burdens become easier to release over time. Practiced pride and arrogance can only serve us for so long. Be grateful for moments of pure discovery, clarity, and release. Every heartbeat is a reminder of home. The journey unfolds in the space between.

Solvitur ambulando

ON SUFFERING

If we give in to suffering, its current will carry us, as it always does — down and away from presence, away from now, into the depths of despair and disconnection.

But if we pause, if we recognize the trigger — that subtle nudge toward the edge — we can stop the spiral before it begins. In that moment of awareness, we can defuse the noise and rise above it, reframing suffering as a teacher rather than a tyrant. With courage, we can grasp the root of the weed and pull it free, clearing the soil for new life to seed.

Suffering is, at its core, a perspective — a lens shaped by our beliefs, fears, and the heavy shadows of guilt, shame, and self-reproach. Yet, it also holds the potential to be something more: a portal to healing, an invitation to transformation.

This shift in perception may feel unnatural at first, running against the grain of cultural conditioning. But like any practice of the heart, it becomes second nature with time, opening the way to lightness, growth, and renewal.

Per dolorem renovamur

WHAT THE HEART WANTS

The desires of your heart are not fleeting whims but whispers of truth, calling you toward deeper resonance — toward who you are and what you are here to become.

. . .

Honor the quiet compass of your longing. Acknowledge it. Appreciate it. Listen to the yearning that stirs your spirit and guides your way. These emotions are vital — signals of resonance that reflect how fully you are, or are not, embodying your truth.

We've been taught to look outward for fulfillment, to chase approval, happiness, or purpose in the noise of the world. We trust the polished reflections of others more than the raw truths buried beneath old wounds and practiced masks. And here, scarcity and lack creep in — anchoring us to the stories of yesterday.

Needs are real, as are yearning and desire, the raw sparks of creation. But their meaning lies in the why and how of their expression. Without awareness, desire twists — a projection, a shield, a chain.

This is why we must breathe. To pause. To discern. To listen for the subtle pull of the helmsman within — the guide who steadies the ship of our lives, even as the storms howl and threaten.

The heart wants what it wants. And beneath all the noise, it already knows the way.

Veritas in corde vivit

LOVE IS LOVE

Love is love — bound by no doctrine, shaped by no dogma, yet it outlasts them all.

To us, it feels like a paradox, forever swaying between want and need, giving and receiving. Conditioned by culture, clouded by ignorance, and colored by arrogance, we often fail to grasp its pure and uncompromising essence. We misuse it, misinterpret it, misdirect it — and too often, we miss it altogether.

We try to contain it, to bind it with words, rituals, obligations, and traditions. We paint it with the strokes of religion and paradigm, wielding both heavy hands and delicate brushes in a futile attempt to control its form.

Yet love is none of these things, though it may touch them all. It is unyielding and unbound — a transcendent force that liberates, invites, and endures. Ego, power, and harm are not its flaws but the shadows we cast in its absence. These shadows are neither righteous nor wicked; they simply are.

Love is the universal yes, the infinite embrace. Ever patient, it waits for us to remember the rhythm and return to the dance.

Amor vincit omnia

Soul Expression

Holding back, suppressing, silencing the raw truth of who you are serves no one.

Your tears cleanse, they heal. Your anger disrupts, reveals, awakens, and stirs the stagnant waters. Your nature — vast, incomparable, fierce in its love — is untamed, dynamic, unrelenting in its truth.

How can you know the breadth of your being or the depth of your longing if you never stretch beyond the familiar, sharpen your gifts, or venture into uncharted passions?

Pleasantries may smooth the surface, but too often, they ring hollow — polite veneers masking quiet desperation. To fake your way through life is to betray yourself, feeding a slow poison that numbs the soul and fragments the mind. This self-denial breeds arrogance, apathy, and a false sense of control, all tools of the parasitic ego.

But this is not who you are.

You are an immortal, divine spark — a master of love, a shaper of light, an artist of infinite creation, and a dreamer commanding vast worlds into being.

So be true. Be real. Be free.

Solvitur ambulando

CLOSE AND FAR AWAY

When I was learning to drive, my mother, a driving instructor at the time, often reminded me, "Look close and look far away." Metaphors abound in the everyday.

Just as on the road, we must regularly check in with our heart — our inner compass — to realign with what we truly desire. Nobody else holds the wheel, and a meaningful journey demands both discipline and a playful sense of awareness. To navigate well, we must be our own best allies — listening, feeling, and ready to adjust course when needed.

But we cannot steer effectively without knowing our destination. Clarity of purpose arises from what ignites us — the passion that needs no reminder to burn. We uncover it through contemplation, imagination, and deliberate action, moving steadily toward our desires with the confidence that what truly matters will unfold in its own time.

Still, the journey's unfolding remains a mystery — and perhaps that's how it's meant to be. This is the gift of conscious awareness: being fully present, even in life's routine or mundane moments, clears away energetic and emotional clutter, stripping us of unnecessary attachments. What remains is the why — the force that sustains our ambition and propels us forward.

You'll know you're on the right path when you feel ecstatic, nervous, joyful, and alive with wide-eyed anticipation.

Look close, and look far away.

Solvitur ambulando

METANOIA: ON CONNECTION

In the modern era, we've lost touch with the depth of human expression. Filters replace authenticity, and fragmented interactions erode the presence and harmony essential for true connection, healing, and growth.

. . .

Distraction is constant, busyness relentless, and passions are pursued with fleeting fervor but little depth. We let the game define the rules and lose ourselves in its demands. It's time to return to the present moment and recapture what's been lost.

We've grown dependent on clunky, mind-numbing technology — paying exorbitant prices for the latest upgrade while tethered to electricity and networks. No charge, no signal — no connection. When was the last time you truly talked to someone — not to complain but to connect? When was the last time you listened fully, without distraction? Conversations have devolved into emojis, grunts, and shallow exchanges, while social media amplifies noise over meaning.

Texting may give us time to collect our thoughts, but it also fosters self-censorship and erodes authenticity. How can we hold real space for others when connection depends on signal strength and fleeting attention spans?

We've lost the courage to speak with our full, resonant voices and the presence to listen beyond soundbites. Instead, we skim life for highlights, craving shortcuts over substance. How did we, as adults, lose the joyful simplicity of a child saying "I love you" with joyful abandon?

Our bodies reflect this disconnection — tight shoulders, shallow chest breaths, and blocked energy centers. Thin skin and inflated egos lead to addictions and neuroses, masking symptoms without addressing the root cause. Trust feels elusive, and healing, unattainable.

To heal, we must rediscover our music — our internal harmony. Connection begins within; we cannot explore vulnerability in isolation.

We all hurt. We all love. We all walk — and learn as we go.

Solvitur ambulando

THE BATTLE INSIDE

You can't have it both ways. The mind will do its thing, and the heart will wait. They are two distinct languages, often at odds with each other.

The mind, however, is the only one ever trying to masquerade as the other.

We can cleverly use logic and reason to make choices, and even go forth to do, try to be, or wish to have, but the feelings, stirrings, intuitions, and emotions seek to guide us truthfully.

Patience, presence, and silence.

In corde veritas

IN THE END

When life comes to reclaim the raw materials,
the choosing is done.

We may have our wits, our memories, our stories,
and our lessons.

We may have family.
We may even leave a legacy.

There's much to decipher, decode, and deliberate upon
while life is in constant motion.

We mustn't lose ourselves in the noise.

ON ARTISTS: SPARKS AND SILENCE

Creativity is a journey of immersion — a dance between inspiration and uncertainty. As artists, we're drawn to something greater, something intangible, but often hesitate at the threshold, reluctant to step into the unknown. The truth is, the magic doesn't lie in perfection or certainty. It lives in the act of beginning — embracing the messiness, the mistakes, and the discoveries along the way.

. . .

As artists, when we dawdle, we quickly become bored, frustrated, or defeated. The magic — the creative spark — has a will of its own, waiting to pull us deeply into the journey. But we must take the reins and embrace the uncertainty.

When I immerse myself in something, I want all of it. I want to learn as much as I can, as quickly as I can. It might even seem obsessive, but this kind of immersion is where rapid learning happens. It's like a character study that a professional actor might undertake. They dive deep to prepare for a role, not just putting on a costume, but adopting the traits, behaviors, and language of their character.

But as artists, those of us who choose a potentially volatile, unpredictable path, we're not merely pretending or temporarily acquiring skills. Instead, we use this process to integrate something meaningful — something that becomes a lasting part of us, enhancing our creative outlets for life. It's transformation, not just preparation. It's character-building, not a transient identity worn to act out a few scenes.

It's important to follow that excitement wherever it leads — to screw up early, make plenty of mistakes, and keep absorbing, molding, and reshaping. Mistakes are the stepping stones of mastery. For those of us who pick things up quickly, persistence and discipline can feel like heavy burdens, even impossible to maintain. The danger lies in letting the pursuit — the art —

become tedious, repetitive work. But repetition is how we solidify knowledge, refine our skills, and truly develop our talents. We cannot simply think ourselves into mastery.

Growth takes time, especially when we work inconsistently — engaging in periods of intensity and obsession with reckless abandon, then shifting gears to rest, waiting for the next spark, intuitive impulse, or external trigger to inspire us to express something with immediacy. Many things in life require patience to fully grasp, integrate, and appreciate, and artists often struggle with this. Our skills and abilities evolve slowly, often imperceptibly. It often takes an objective perspective from someone else to remind us of how far we've come.

In music, our ears continue to mature. In photography, our eyes grow sharper. In writing, our words, language, and authenticity deepen. In film, we refine our storytelling and master the art of capturing light in motion, weaving hundreds or thousands of moments into a cohesive vision — and then hoping it will resonate with an audience. In carpentry or construction, our hands become steadier, and our use of tools more precise. Across every creative pursuit, the process is one of constant refinement and maturation — a lifelong evolution.

With vivid imaginations, immense empathy, and a hunger for high-intensity creative processes, we artists often fall prey to overthinking. It's easy to paralyze ourselves. But the magic lies in the act of creating — in the purity of losing ourselves to the process, the spiritual expansion, the mental exploration, and the depth of discovery found in the present moment — not in endlessly pondering where to begin or where the journey may lead.

Trust the flow. Go, create.

Solvitur ambulando

On Service: You're Enough

The great lesson to learn of life is the need of giving
out from the abundance of one's self in order to be
ever abundant within one's self.

— Walter Russell

We move through life often blind to the ripples we create — quiet acts
of care, unnoticed efforts, and the energy we share. Yet, it is these
unassuming moments that can shape someone's world, even as we
underestimate our own.

. . .

We often dismiss our efforts, especially the small ones. We
undervalue our positive impact on others because of how we
perceive ourselves and frame our worldview. We color the canvas
with preconceptions, paradigmatic programming, and assumptions
about how others see us — our worth, our contribution, or even
our existence.

When we feel we're not enough, nothing we do feels like enough.
We are too hard on ourselves and often forget that everyone shares
the same concerns, worries, and struggles. We simply use different
words and scenarios to describe them.

It's overcomplicated. The spirit's nature is to serve, yet the noise in
our minds — fueled by the stories and traumas we've lived —
creates a heaviness in the chest, solar plexus, or belly. It can
manifest as headaches, tighten our throats, suppress our sexuality,
and stifle our creatorship. These patterns needlessly diminish our
expressions of love, willpower, and energetic sensitivity. The mind's
chaotic rhythm has little to do with who we truly are. Conforming
to its endless cacophony can be paralyzing, compelling us to look
down and away. It undermines connection, authenticity, and —
most importantly — vulnerability.

When the human race learns how to give and regive equally each will be enriched. He who withholds that which he should give to another impoverishes both himself and the other.

— Walter Russell

Meet the eyes of those you care for. Recognize that gratitude is a vortex of co-creation — an expansive vibration that benefits everyone. Allow your mind to spin as it will, but you stay here: see the fruits of your labor as valuable and useful. Observe how encouragement ignites a spark. Recognize that just listening is often enough. Simply being present in effortless quiet is grounding. It holds space and requires no training whatsoever.

It may sound like an oversimplification, but it remains true: just be yourself. We do not step into the lives of others by accident, nor is the life we chose an accident. You are given limitless love, talent, and creativity. Regive it.

Solvitur ambulando

WHAT WE CARRY, WHAT WE LET GO

Sometimes, the weight we carry feels unbearable, yet within this discomfort lies an invitation — to pause, reflect, and alchemize resistance into growth, revealing a clearer path forward.

. . .

Tension can build so sharply within us that blinders rise, the heart locks down, the stomach twists, and the mind and body ache. It feels paralyzing, yet this very discomfort signals an opportunity: to confront lingering resistance and uncover the growth that may be hidden in its release.

In these moments, we face a choice — to surrender to frustration or to channel its energy into transformation. A stranger's words, a passing insight, or even an overheard fragment of conversation can shift our perspective, sparking a cascade of revelation and renewal.

Vulnerability often leads us to clarity. When the weight becomes too much to bear, our inner compass — the heart and spirit — insists that we release what no longer serves, clearing space for movement and meaning.

We pile immense pressure upon ourselves, layering societal expectations over our personal ambitions and desires. Yet, beneath this clutter lies the authentic self, waiting to emerge. Struggle is inevitable, but not all struggles deserve our time or energy. Periodically, we must pause to question what we value, discarding outdated goals and beliefs that hinder our growth. What is your why?

Simplify. Loosen your grip on the irrelevant. Growth is not a grand leap — it's the next small, intentional step toward self-awareness and authenticity.

Temet nosce

THE CONSCIOUSNESS

The road before
And behind
Is weathered with seasons
Storms and
Flash floods
Sprinkled with silence
A pregnant mist
The utterly serene
And timeless…

While we may indeed
Tend to favor
The dramatic
It is in the essence
Of this place
That we violently
Shape and shift
The ethereal
Intangible
Untraceable
Into the transitive
Temporance
Of integrity…

We certainly needn't
Take a bite
Out of life
For life meets us exactly
With the intensity with which
We dare
To engage it…

But if the entire point
Of love divine
Is to explore eternity
There are no roads

Nor fractal passages
Save the one
We are on
Right
Now…

HARD FEELINGS

We must be willing to feel into the hard places
Or the shadow will persist
Muting the magnificent
Paling the present
Bouncing us out of the musical groove
Time and again

We cannot don the immersive sensuality of
Fullness, richness and
Depth of the everything
If we believe we can compartmentalize
Pain, growth, and healing

Try as we might (and mightily in madness)
Pushing the pedal to the floor
While the soul is in idle
Only serves to burn the reserves
And pollute our environment

Let love lead and
Trust your truth to emerge

It Just Shows Up

One doesn't go looking for their art
As one doesn't go looking for love
It just shows up
The work is in honing the rudiments
Refining skills
Communication and
Listening
Clearing and cleansing
The mechanism
But always and forever
Most of all
Opening the heart
The truest space of the creative

So Be It

Be it so gentle
that an uttered word
would shatter the dream

Be it so subtle
that the breath of fire
would blow harmlessly past

Be it so complete
that even the question
would ignite a great war

Be it so beautiful
that its discovery
would finish the book

Be it so peaceful
that even a waveless ocean
would envy the calm

Love: so be it

LOSE YOURSELF IN IT

Music has always been a thread woven through the fabric of my life, pulling me back to moments both vivid and forgotten. The memories it stirs are as random as they are profound, often triggered by the simplest things.

. . .

I recall several unforgettable moments in my life that revolved around music. It's fascinating how seemingly random memories surface, tethered to whatever occupies our minds at a given time.

When I was ten or eleven, we lived in a house with a detached garage behind it. My father had built a small music room there, where I set up my first drum kit. It became a rehearsal space for our family band, which played at the Croatian club and other venues for several years. We practiced in that tiny room, but as always, my favorite moments were spent alone.

During those solo jam sessions, I began discovering my singing voice — even though it was often drowned out by the thunderous chaos of live drums. To hear myself, I had to sing at the top of my lungs, unabashed and free from the worry of volume control. It was liberating. With no one listening, I could close my eyes, sink into a rhythm, and completely lose myself in the music. Any artist will tell you this is why they create: to transcend the present moment, suspend time, and dissolve into their chosen medium. And when the dust of creation settles, they hope something remains — something meaningful to share with the world.

At the time, my drum kit was a mismatched assortment — some parts were Ludwig, some were generic. I didn't care, nor did I know much about brands, tunings, or even matching drumsticks. None of it mattered because I could make music with anything. To this day, my voice remains one of my favorite instruments.

I still remember the smells of that room — the dust, the faint tang of fermenting wine, and the mustiness of timeworn gear. My father's equipment from his 1970s band days sat among wine bottles and winemaking tools. The floor was covered with old shag carpet, and the drywall bore stains from a fermenting demijohn that had popped its top under pressure. Acoustically, the space was terrible. But for an intensely introverted soul, it was a sanctuary — a place to release creative energy and escape the distractions of the outside world.

Years later, while working in a studio, I had the chance to record and produce my first albums. I was self-taught, as always, and the steep learning curve was as thrilling as it was challenging. I'll never forget those nights when the sun would set and rise again as I worked on mixes, arrangements, and backing vocals. Sleep seemed irrelevant; I was too immersed in the work to feel tired.

In hindsight, those moments remind me how vital it is to carve out time and space for our true selves. Life has a way of overwhelming us with busyness, much of it unnecessary. The moments we remember most vividly are those when we stop overthinking and simply are — fully present. That's where the magic lies.

But life often pulls us away from this magic. It's not that every breath we take isn't its own tiny miracle, but we don't always live with that level of awareness. The world, with its relentless demands and distractions, constantly asks for more — more of our attention, more of our energy. If we're not careful, it can steal from us the most precious parts of this fleeting existence.

So, whenever we can, we should reclaim that magic. Create a sanctuary, however small, where you can lose yourself in something meaningful. Whether it's making music, writing, or simply being still, give yourself permission to dissolve into the moment. The world will wait.

Musica est vita

Storm Winds

It was a stormy, windy night when the island's power went out yet again. I found myself wondering about the trees — and who the hell was flying that prop plane slowly cruising overhead — while the big, bright ferry sat parked at the terminal across the narrows.

But the trees were far more interesting. I imagined them reveling in the storm, dancing wildly in the wind, exuberantly shouting "Yyyyyeeeaaaahhh!" and "Wheeeeeee!" (in tree language, of course). They've spent the majority of their lives standing calm and strong, unhurried. All of that spiraling and branching must have been done with the awareness that they'd be tested regularly by the elements.

I wonder if there's a collective "Hooray!" when one of them falls — snapped in half or blown over to reveal its roots. Do the others nearby celebrate their friend's dramatic and glorious exit?

I've always loved windstorms. Well, any storm, really. Thunder and lightning hold a particularly intense energy. As a young boy, I loved climbing the tree in our front yard, especially when the wind picked up. It wasn't a massive cedar or spruce like the seasoned adventurers outside my window now, living here in coastal British Columbia. But it was tall enough to sway in a good breeze, and I'd climb all the way to the top. Enveloped by the overwhelming torrent of sound and movement, it felt magical.

And when this storm passes, as storms always do, the rains will come to wash away the dust. We'll step over some debris, looking for the guilty parties. Those trees will no doubt just stand there innocently and stoically, perhaps muttering, "Nothing to see here. Carry on."

"Oh? Then why are you glowing?"

Nature amazes.

Slowly, We Build: On Trust

In the quiet spaces between what we say and what we mean, trust takes root. It doesn't come quickly or without effort, but slowly, like the first light of dawn breaking through the dark — steady, patient, and inevitable.

. . .

Trusting someone with your pain is never easy. Just as unrealistic is expecting them to trust you with theirs. These things take time. When we misinterpret the words or actions of those we care about, we're often quick to leap to negative conclusions. Instead of rushing to judgment, we can choose to pause, hold space, and let things unfold naturally. Trust isn't built in a moment, nor is it something we can force.

Relationships, like anything meaningful, require patience and care. You can't build walls on a freshly poured foundation. If the foundation is laid during the rain or in winter's chill, it takes even longer to set. So, why rush? What's the point of hurrying through something that deserves to be done right? Relationships thrive not on speed but on strength — the kind of strength that comes from a steady, unwavering commitment to laying the groundwork with care and intention.

We live in a culture obsessed with speed and instant gratification. We want everything now, and when it comes to relationships, we often bring the same impatient mindset. Emotional immaturity thrives in this environment, manifesting as overthinking, obsessing, or endlessly seeking validation. But love and adoration are not fleeting emotions. They're profound, steady forces that require depth and patience to grow.

In our relentless race to go nowhere, we've lost sight of so much that is sacred. We skim, scroll, and rush through life, treating even the most meaningful aspects with a kind of transactional urgency. But the essence of life — the true beauty of it — lies in the pauses.

It's in the deliberate, mindful moments when we stop to reflect and engage deeply.

Think of a book. Its cover offers only an impression, a fleeting glimpse of what lies within. The synopsis may hint at the themes, but the real substance, the heart of it, is hidden in its pages. You can't rush the experience of reading if you truly want to understand the story. The same is true of living. Take your time. Read deeply. Live fully. Pause to reflect, and then step forward again with renewed understanding.

When the moment feels right, share what you've learned. What you discover in those quiet, reflective spaces might not only transform your own life but also be the very wisdom someone else is waiting to hear. And in that exchange, a sacred connection is forged — one built not on speed or convenience, but on the enduring strength of authenticity and understanding.

Love your life

SOCIAL BEINGS

In a world where our digital consumption shapes our perceptions, we must learn to navigate the noise and reconnect with the deeper currents of truth and human connection.

. . .

Our media feeds pulse endlessly, shaping our perception of reality in ways we rarely notice. By curating what we consume, we create insular bubbles — filtering out perspectives that challenge us, often without realizing it. The content we engage with signals the algorithm, which then serves up more of the same, reinforcing familiar beliefs and patterns. But what are we missing, even from those we admire or align with? Naturally, we gravitate toward what feels comfortable, avoiding contradictions to our values and views. Yet, to truly understand, we must embrace the discomfort of exploring the other side of the story.

While original ideas may be rare, what crosses our path often holds messages that resonate. We want to see the world improve, but the ceaseless stream of dramatic and negative news can leave us agitated and overwhelmed. The world often defaults to its darker tendencies — a sobering reality we cannot ignore.

There's an irony here: despite being more connected than ever, the digital age has birthed a profound loneliness. We're always online, yet increasingly isolated — hiding behind screens, usernames, and avatars. In these virtual spaces, we can choose to amplify extremes, disengage, or retreat entirely. But no matter how we navigate this digital realm, one truth remains: we cannot escape ourselves, nor should we.

We are social beings, made for collaboration and creative expression. It's encouraging to see vulnerability and honesty emerge in online conversations, yet the richness of life's most meaningful experiences cannot be replaced by pixels and posts.

There is immense power in disconnecting — in stepping away from the screens and into the stillness of life. Set boundaries for yourself. Find solace in quiet withdrawal, whether through reading, writing, or simply sitting in silence.

And when the world feels too loud, gather. Sit by a campfire with loved ones, sharing stories and laughter under a canopy of stars. In these simple, unfiltered moments, we reclaim what it means to truly connect.

Love your life

A Great Debate: On Discourse

*True dialogue is an art — a delicate balance of expression and
listening, shaped by curiosity and respect. Yet, in today's world, this
art is all but lost, replaced by echo chambers and endless contention.
We're not merely talking past one another; we're losing the ability to
connect, to challenge, and to grow together. It's time we remember
that meaningful conversation isn't about winning — it's about
understanding.*

. . .

Engaging in paradigm-shifting dialogue is nearly impossible when
everyone assumes they're right. This creates a childish heaviness —
ineffective at best, destructive at worst. Discourse and debate have
devolved into ad hominem attacks and verbal sparring designed to
provoke rather than connect. It's rarely, if ever, a meeting of the
minds.

To move forward as a collective, we must temper knee-jerk
reactions and ground our concerns in compassion, heart-centered
listening, and patience. This calls for emotional maturity — simple
in theory but exceedingly rare in practice. Some might argue it has
been systematically suppressed, dulled by an increasingly
compromised and ideologically driven public education system.

But here's a question: do you practice patience, compassion, and
deep listening even with yourself? Is it kind, considerate, or
empowering to relentlessly criticize and shame yourself for who
you are, what you do, or what you have?

This isn't about political debate; this is about real life. Being truly
present is crucial. The endless cycle of historical revisionism,
narrative manipulation, media spin, and propaganda only amplifies
the noise. These paid actors and constructed personas should be
made irrelevant — not because they lack truth, but because the
authority we grant them enables profound harm. Fixating on them
— in public discourse or private conversations — provides a

convenient scapegoat, a moving target onto which we project our collective frustrations. It's always *their* fault, isn't it?

Yet, in doing so, we unknowingly allow these fabricated characters to influence us. Their behavior becomes the baseline, shaping a culture of division, chaos, and blame.

Genuine dialogue transcends this. It interrogates ideologies, moves beyond fictitious lines on empire-drawn maps, and rises above the clamor of manipulated narratives to challenge the status quo. True discussions elevate us — they're love and passion in motion.

We are one heartbeat, calling ourselves human, sharing this Earth and the sunlight that sustains us. Love isn't logical or measurable, but it binds us. It is the glue of purpose, the essence of our *ikigai*, and the stepping stone to unity consciousness — if we choose to embody and walk that path.

Honest discourse unveils deeper truths. It beckons us to move beyond curated, censored forums into expansive, genuine conversations. What lies on the edges of our intuition invites us toward light — open, present, and life-affirming. To engage in this dance of reciprocity, we need only adjust our frequency to match.

It starts with you. Elevate.

Ego relinque, veritatem amplectere

Community

Share your experiences — the triumphs and the trials, the struggles and the breakthroughs. Those who walk ahead, beside, and behind you on this journey will find inspiration in your courage and authenticity.

Though we each weave threads into the grand narrative, your perspective is uniquely yours. Embrace it. Grow through it. Teach as you learn, and learn as you teach.

We honor one another by stepping into vulnerability and exploring life with intention. Your voice matters. Your truth is needed.

Solvitur ambulando

THE GENTLE HAND

There's a quiet force in the still moments we often overlook as life pulses around us. It's easy to be swept up in the noise — chasing what's next, or clinging to what's past. Yet the deeper truths lie in the pauses, in the spaces between thoughts, where the heart beats unencumbered.

. . .

Even amid life's most violent episodes, subtleties are at work. Life unfolds not in chaos, but in the serene, unhurried flow of the organic — the natural rhythm of existence. We navigate this realm through a interplay of forces, both immense and delicate.

To live fully in the present requires a willingness to let go of time and place. The now is shaped by cycles of tension and release, disintegration and renewal. Life asks us to complete each of these cycles, granting ourselves the closure we need, both spiritually and psychologically. Until we reintegrate the parts of ourselves trapped in limbo — fragmented, caged in attachments, or lost to the past — we obstruct the flow of life and mire its motion.

Life will not allow us to idle without consequence. Resistance to its current brings suffering, obscuring our purpose and deferring our calling — our *ikigai* — no matter what distractions or coping mechanisms we employ.

This is not how industry and commerce work. Those who labor, create, and innovate — who tinker, compose, research, sculpt, paint, or write — are often undervalued. Meanwhile, those in glass towers manipulate odds and amass wealth without creating anything of substance or uplifting others. True reparations for this imbalance may never come, but it need not trouble us. This disparity reflects the values of a lesser paradigm, reminding us that we are living differently — living better.

Our focus must remain on individuation, on embracing our unique mission and purpose, trusting that life will sustain us. The world is shaped by those who have the patience, courage, and fortitude to heed the gentle hand's guidance — not merely to survive, but to thrive, to create, and to pursue their dreams with abandon, regardless of material reward. As they nurture their creativity, they teach the collective the meaning of authenticity. As they live their truth, they embody imagination and character over illusion and pretense.

The gentle hand lifts our chins, no matter how often we stumble. It urges us to reach in for the kiss, to extend a hand, to write the book, or to paint the sky. It nurtures our failures and mistakes, encouraging us to make more. This hand — our higher self, our inner knowing, the spark of our source-field — is unbiased yet wholly aligned with our spirit.

Whatever form or function we are meant to serve, this world has space for it. We shine brightest in our own skin, for there are infinite shades of light, and every one of them matters.

In via tua veritas

ONE TRUE VOICE

Play on, you symphony of madness. Blast the horns counter to the rhythm, rake the strings with angst and anxiety. Pound the timpani with closed fists for all I care. You won't slow me down now.

I can hear the one true voice, resonant and solely relevant, regardless of your redundant crowd of dissonance. Like a bell fabricated of my own essence, she sings clearly to me across the waves, through the corridors and bracing my heart.

I am here, and on my island, all at once; renewed.

I am that divine love. I am with you.

BLOODLETTING

Truth is the pricker of thin skin; authenticity lets the blood flow.

Face your dark, beautiful self.

Embrace him.

Let her go.

These shadows are echoes, stories, and seeds long sown.

Now begins the new chapter, destination unknown.

ECHOES OF A FORGOTTEN FREEDOM

At some point, we all realize that the weight we carry isn't entirely our own, and the patterns we follow aren't always of our design. As children, we lived in the freedom to explore, to wonder, to leap without looking. But somewhere along the way, the world taught us to conform. Now, as the tide shifts and the foundations we've built on begin to crack, we are called to reconnect with that childlike curiosity — that raw, unfiltered sense of adventure.

. . .

With time and reflection, it becomes easier to be honest with ourselves. As we journey through life, the dots begin to connect, the storylines align, and with that comes a deeper understanding of our struggles and perceptions — perhaps even a renewed clarity.

It's fascinating to recall our instinctive freedom as children. We felt the pull of excitement and dove in without hesitation, unconcerned with schedules, validation, or whether something would earn us a living. Curiosity, openness, adventure, and a willingness to fail were natural states of being. Left to our own devices, we would dare greatly, again and again.

But those who raised us — parents, guardians, and institutions — often battling their own quests for validation and meaning, begrudged us our independence. Through their examples and influence, they eroded and suppressed our innocence, our passion, and our play. Trust in our internal compasses faded as exploration was segmented, controlled, and dictated by schedules, alarms, and demands.

Out of a desire to serve and please those we cared about — or perhaps even feared — we forged allegiances with those who had already abandoned the pursuit of a genuinely well-lived life. Form, function, logic, and emotional detachment became the norm, and we accepted it.

120

But now, we are standing on the edge of a new existence, shaking our foundations to the core. All our systems — every one of them — must evolve, adapt, or be replaced entirely. This destabilizes the parasitic unconscious and unnerves the power-hungry manipulators who thrive on control. As a species, we are no longer able to function as we once did; our vibratory and energetic expressions have fundamentally shifted and quickened.

We owe it to ourselves to pause, to reconnect with our essential selves — free from makeup, titles, labels, expectations, or time constraints. To simply inhabit the naked now.

If we can be bold enough to do this, we might reboot the stagnating processes within us, breaking apart the calcified layers of impositions and external influence. Regaining the presence and perseverance to overcome these soul-crushing forces is the challenge of our time.

And there, waiting, is the excitement. The curiosity. The openness. The adventure. There, we'll rediscover the willingness to reveal, to sail, to soar — free of the unruly heaviness.

That forgotten dream, that childlike freedom, was never truly lost. It has only been waiting for us to remember.

Vivat miratio

An Artist's Way

An artist must choose to shun acceptable behavior, political correctness, and the comforts of the commonplace to truly exist in the spacetime of their genius. Playing it safe is like painting by numbers, stealing a riff, using pitch correction, obeying the clock, failing, failing again, and then giving up; it's pandering to the normals and ignoring what the world desperately needs from us.

It's not that we seek out the pain, but that it's the shortest path back to the truth. Only in that space do we find the surest way to lose ourselves in the glorious, timeless moment of pure, thoughtless abandon. We crave that honest ecstasy, yet we die with every breath we keep it at arm's length — relegated to a task list, forever in limbo. The longer we put it off, the more inequitable our lives feel.

We chose the artist's way. We chose to be raw, sensitive, unpredictable, counter-commonplace, and counter-intuitive. We are the other half of the scale that holds this reality in balance. It's our onus to remember, now and then, that we have intrinsic value here.

You be you.

Via artis vera est

FEAR, IN MOTION

You can use your fear to recharge yourself. Truly. It can drain you, crash your energy, or be transmuted into fuel for creative, inspired action.

In every breath, love.

Solvitur ambulando

ON MASTERY: THE ART OF BECOMING

The journey of learning is rarely linear. It twists and turns, filled with leaps of inspiration, stretches of doubt, and moments of clarity that seem to emerge from nowhere. It's not about mastering every step but about showing up — raw, curious, and willing to fail — trusting that the process will shape us into who we are meant to become.

. . .

They say it takes around 10,000 hours to master anything — a musical instrument, a language, a trade, or a sport. In my own journey, I've found this to hold true, uncovering valuable insights along the way. While I don't know if I've truly mastered anything, I've delved deeply into various pursuits, learning as I go.

In structured education, we follow predictable curricula with set expectations. And we pay for it, often at a significant cost. Over a defined period, instructors guide us through the basics and beyond, aiming for certification. This approach provides consistency, focus, and guidance, steering us toward our aspirations. It's rigorous but foundational, shaping us into the people we strive to become.

But what happens when we forgo formal education? As autodidacts, we become our own mentors and motivators. This self-guided path can be harsh, especially for artists who often wrestle with chronic self-criticism. There may be no upfront financial cost, but we pay a different price over time. Art is a wild force, both tormenting and transformative. Yet embracing its challenges is where true growth occurs.

In school, feedback is immediate, correcting mistakes and preventing bad habits. This structured environment suits those seeking predictable, linear career paths. By contrast, the independent route offers no such certainty. Skills are entirely self-made, born of effort, happy accidents, and imagination. This freedom is exhilarating but isolating — though for some, solitude is essential for uncovering truth and pursuing authenticity.

In a competitive world, independence can feel like both a blessing and a curse. "Making a living" often carries a heavy connotation, especially when creative confidence falters. Watching others succeed — their popularity, marketability, and appeal — can lead us to question our worth.

The key is openness, flexibility, and receptiveness to life's unexpected opportunities. When excitement and passion fuel experimentation and craft, that energy resonates with those who value and support our work. For the independent, living with uncertainty fosters resilience and self-reliance.

Today, we can learn almost anything, anywhere, in any way we choose. Yet the same questions persist: Can we motivate ourselves? Trust our efforts? Believe in their worth? The freedom to create and align with our true selves is ours, but it demands uncommon discipline, self-awareness, and personal accountability — all while trusting life's flow.

Above all, we must be gentle with ourselves, stay curious, and embrace the journey. No one else can live our story or offer the world what we uniquely bring.

Be yourself, beautiful soul. Thank you for your courage, your vulnerability, and your authenticity. Thank you for your love of art, your art of love, your unique perspective, and for sharing your true self with us.

Solvitur ambulando

Wayshower: In the Footsteps of Time

We are all travelers here, walking paths both worn and wild, sculpted by the choices we've made. The world, in all its beauty and chaos, is a mirror — reflecting back the shadows and light we've yet to fully understand. Each step forward is both a revelation and a riddle, a call to remember something ancient and untold within us, a dance between what is and what could be. To journey is to become the question and the answer, to step into the unknown and claim it as our own.

. . .

It is the plight of the wayshowers to battle the winds of time and clear the path for those who follow. There are no victims here; we choose our adventure with every breath, between every heartbeat. When we embraced the skills and senses of the uncommon and elevated, we invited the necessary process of training and refinement. We all have our strengths, and we all carry latent abilities — understandings that will find their time, their place, and their worldly purpose. The cycles and spirals of this dance will ensure it.

We may choose accidents or circumstances, the unexpected or the methodical. It doesn't matter. Each of us carries a brilliance within, a soul's light that fits intuitively, perfectly, always. The machines of this world have pounded it down, drumming relentlessly, but we, too, had a hand in their design. We are rhythm masters, employing all things as reasons and rudiments to explore both in front of and behind the veil.

We may look at the darker ages as stumbling stones we all tripped over and were injured by. Yet, if we consider the vastness of forever, those ages — those moments — occurred not only overnight but in less than the blink of an eye, a fraction of that.

We seem content to accept the plodding pace of history as it's been recorded, taking to heart what is merely a superficial and woefully incomplete narrative. This instills a sense of doldrum, a melancholy weighed down by neverendingness, set upon us by the illusion of time's fatigue.

But we forget: the nature of our reality allows for an elastic pull to dark extremes, not as punishment but as preparation for an equal and opposite thrust toward light. This dynamic tension, though painful, is the universe's way of exploring balance and revealing hidden truths. The struggles we endure — the losses, detours, and moments of despair — are not random; they are the catalysts that shape us, calling us to integrate what was broken and reclaim what was forgotten. Inevitably, we see how even the darkest moments served a purpose, moving us closer to wholeness and the fullness of who we are.

We can expend much energy blaming the iniquity of the tripping stones and judging relentlessly the alleged fools who've fallen in the same way for countless generations. Our pain needs a drum to beat, and we will continue looking "out there" for enemies, for prophecies — and especially for conspiracies. But until we welcome it home — until we have the grace to embrace our fragments and dislocated selves — we remain unwhole, wanting, shaken, unsafe, defensive, incomplete.

We are here now, in this moment, to recapitulate and amend the story. Everywhere, there is evidence of the shift — an acceleration into lightness and harmony as the elastic coils pull us from the depths of the extinct into the extant spirit.

Lead on. Light the way. Time is irrelevant, as is its impatience, the literal fatigue it imposes upon us. This has always been a place of feeling, where love knows no bounds.

Remember?

Via veritatis, via lucis

Opposite Pain

*Your pain is the breaking of the shell that encloses
your understanding.*

— Kahlil Gibran

*We are all walking contradictions, caught between the pull of what
we've known and the call of what we've yet to become. Each moment
is a fracture in time, a space where the past whispers and the future
beckons. In this delicate balance, we find both the weight of what
holds us down and the lightness of what could lift us. The tension
between these forces is where we learn, where we grow, and where the
deepest truths of our existence are revealed.*

. . .

Pain is one of those four-letter words that encapsulates many
things. It means different things at different times, triggers an
assortment of feelings and emotions, and, ultimately, teaches — it
always offers a lesson. This is the nature of living in a reality
defined by duality and contrast.

Fear and pain are closely intertwined, though the former is
psychological and conceptual, while the latter is primarily physical.
At their core, both are forms of resistance — spiritually and
metaphysically speaking. Resistance turns us away from the flow; it
is anti-life, unconscious action, egoic persistence instead of
heartfelt constancy.

Our world is steeped in fear, pain, and their many derivatives. A
certain numbness pervades our time, for we largely dwell in the
space between. We are unsure of what is worth holding onto and
carrying forward, even as we awaken to the call to elevate our
interconnected existence. This call urges us to embrace ease, grace,
lightness, unity, authenticity, and the deep, naked knowing that
beckons us out of our shadowy, self-sustained caverns.

What lies opposite pain is, understandably, almost unknown. To reach it, we must learn to trust again. Hundreds of generations have relied predominantly on pushing, pulling, fighting, forming, factoring, mapping, manipulating — and being manipulated.

Every eye you meet holds the terror they can't yet voice. Though, as a society, we've become more polarized and compartmentalized, I believe this moment is like an archer's bow being drawn, the slingshot stretched, the catapult cranked tight. This evolutionary conflux is steadying and purifying us, preparing to propel us far beyond the clumsy constructs we've accepted and half-heartedly integrated. We are so much more than this, and the river is about to burst through the dam.

What lies opposite pain is openness. It is tangible, ready for the partaking. It is the breath that rises from your soul. It is knowing — and acting — in alignment with excitement, gratitude, flow, faith, and foresight. It is the vortex that has been amassing your desires, passions, and the unreasonable dreams you've dared to imagine.

It is accepting, perhaps for the first time, that maybe there's nothing wrong with you.

Can you feel it?

Solvitur ambulando

EVERYDAY PRESENCE

It's easy to lose sight of your divinity amidst the humdrum of the everyday. Yet, within the mundane and unassuming, treasures lie hidden — nuggets of pure gold awaiting the spiritually untethered seeker.

These heartbeats will not return, so breathe life into each one.

Embody the moment. Let the fertile emptiness rekindle your flame.

Reclaim it.

Divinum in quotidiano

ADVERSITY

Every moment of adversity calls us to remember the power buried beneath layers of fear and compromise — to break free and reclaim it.

. . .

The saying goes, "Adversity builds character." But let's take it further: adversity challenges accepted limits and demands expansion, drawing on latent strengths that align with our truest selves.

Our society is drowning — in cowardice, fear, superficiality, ideology, and politics. We yield to special interests, more comfortable donning masks and fine clothing while chastising those who dare to live raw, free, and honest. Our collective character is brittle, yet the cracks are beginning to show. Finally, the status quo trembles.

A deeper knowing — our spiritual substance — is stirring. It peacefully protests our complacency, forcing impurities to boil to the surface. Our deepest truth refuses to let us stand idly by. We are in the midst of a vibrational shift, an energy that will not turn back.

This is a cosmic sink-or-swim moment: we must embody the new story — authenticity, heart-centered action, intuition, empathy — or all we hold dear may disappear. We can no longer play along with being played for fools.

Adversity, then, is an omen. It is both an opportunity and a call to enact your soul's will. Heed its pain, but don't be stubborn. Trust the unknown; embrace it. We know, instinctively, right from wrong, love from fear. Our feelings and emotions are guides — but only if we clear the spirals of angst that obscure their wisdom.

We are more than we suppose ourselves to be.

Solvitur ambulando

THE NEW STORY

Start telling the new story.

Stuff will come up — it has to.

Pain and self-sabotage can become routine, an insidious trap that keeps us unconscious if we let it. Entire lifetimes can slip away this way.

Time is irrelevant. Age is irrelevant.

The old story may be valid, but is it still relevant?

Novum initium

The Present We Overlook

We live in a constant tug-of-war between the pull of the future and the stillness of the present. The future is a mirage — a shifting horizon we chase, convinced fulfillment lies just beyond it. Yet, in the chase, we overlook the profound power of now — the only moment we truly have. Everything we seek, every answer we need, is already here, waiting to be uncovered.

. . .

Our obsession with linearity may be our greatest foe. We've constructed a world of restrictions, grinding against the natural flow of life under the illusion of control. These constraints define our physicality and emotional spectrum — they work, but can we grow beyond their spiritual impositions?

We're addicted to the future, caught in an endless loop of planning, scheduling, and conforming. Society hums like a hive of drones, following corporatocratic messaging born of the endless demand for economic growth and so-called progress. We trade our most limited resource — time — for income, saving for education, housing, travel, security, and retirement. Laws, rituals, and ideologies reinforce this cycle, handed down generation after generation. Do we ever stop to ask: is this truly improvement? Do we even know what "better" means anymore? How can we recognize "better" if we've lost our ability to value the present?

The narrative of "hope for the future" is both misleading and disempowering. It defers focus to an ambiguous, nonexistent time and place. "Hope" and "faith" are convenient lies that rationalize suffering and justify impositions we didn't choose. Hope asks for change without action, disguising our inherent power to shape the present.

We've forgotten the extraordinary power of now. It's not found in the distractions of modern life. True foundations exist in family, nature, art, open dialogue, and wild play. These are where life unfolds, where meaning resides.

Anything that pulls you from the present deserves interrogation. Where did it come from? Who does it serve? What else is possible? What would love do? Is it even true?

Listen to the stillness within you. Here. Now.

Tempus fugit, praesens manet

WATER

Water…
So patient
Effortless
The definition of flow
Unresistant
Shape shifting
Life lifting
Ever drifting
Ease
Outlasts the winds
Escapes the fires
Hides in the dirt…
She graces the shore
Composing
An infinite symphony
That pleases me
So easily
Our minds
One
And done
Undone
Water…
So patient

READINESS

We can push
Through the mire
The haze
The mechanics of life

We can fight
With the stream
The flow
The waters of support

Or we can surrender
To the knowing
The trust
The amplified instrument

We can relish
Within the fog
Within the mysterious
Within the ubiquitous love

And remember
The readiness
The anticipation
The definition
Of adventure
Of rapture
Of simply being
Here
Now

Yes

COURAGEOUS HEART

But I will wear my heart upon my sleeve
For daws to peck at: I am not what I am.

— Iago, from Shakespeare's *Othello*

Wearing your heart on your sleeve is an act of courage and
vulnerability, a timeless expression of love in its purest, most
abundant form — unguarded, without fear, judgment, or limits. It
reminds us that love is the invisible thread binding all things and that
the choice to share it freely or withhold it rests solely with us.

. . .

Rooted in chivalry and knighthood, immortalized in stories like
Shakespeare's *Othello*, the phrase "wearing your heart on your
sleeve" reflects a universal truth: to openly express your feelings is
to risk being hurt, misunderstood, or rejected. Yet it is in this raw,
unguarded state that we discover our truest strength — and our
deepest connection to the sacred energy of love.

Love resists control, defies boundaries, and flows abundantly. Yet
we ration it, deciding who is worthy and who is not. What a strange
and unnecessary game — this withholding of something so
limitless, so essential. Love is never in short supply; it is we who
practice restriction, cutting ourselves off from its abundance, from
others, and from ourselves. Can we unlearn this habit?

Vulnerability is strength. It is the quiet power of holding a child's
hand, cherishing a token of a loved one, or creating space for
shared humanity. These simple acts transcend words, reminding us
that love isn't something to measure or reserve — it is something to
embody, moment by moment.

To wear your heart on your sleeve is to dare greatly. It is to
challenge the instinct to protect, to question the judgments and
unconscious walls you've built. It is to stand open in a world that

often demands pretense, masks, and armor. This kind of openness requires bravery — a bravery few are taught but all are capable of cultivating. In this openness, you reclaim your connection to the effortless, abundant flow of life.

Even the deepest pain and the darkest hate are transient. Like waves on the shore, they rise, crest, and fall away. The choice is always yours: to cling to the heaviness or to let it go. To live closed off, or to let love — unguarded and unbound — lead the way.

Amor sine timore

SIMPLY BEING

In a world that constantly demands more — more doing, achieving, and proving — we've lost sight of the power of simply being. The relentless drive for validation blinds us to the quiet strength of presence. Yet, in stillness lies clarity, and in silence, the answers we've been chasing. To rediscover ourselves, we must stop, breathe, and listen to what is already whole within us.

. . .

We are deeply identified with doing — with our egos and the ways society measures our worth through action. This need for constant stimulation drives us to madness, pulling us further from the essence of who we are without titles or accomplishments.

This obsession feeds much of our suffering. Competition, consumerism, and status dominate our lives, entangled with entitlement, shame, cynicism, and apathy. We're consumed by anxieties about debt, social standing, fragile economies, and divisive politics. And so, the cycle continues: we justify endless progress, more consumption, and more waste, all while feeding an emptiness that grows in the shadows.

It's time to break this pattern. To stop passing the madness onto our children. To stop seeking validation through the approval of others — whether family, society, or public opinion. The first step is to reconnect with stillness and allow ourselves to simply be.

Dive inward and meet your inner traveler. Find your center in what truly resonates with you. Meditation, in its many forms, is a path back to presence — for yourself, for those you love, and for those yet to come. We've overcomplicated life, veiled our emotions, and eroded trust. It's time to simplify. The art of being requires shedding the layers of conditioning we adopted without thought.

"I can't afford to stop."

No — you can't afford not to.

All these things we labor to maintain have become our masters. What is your truth? Your passion? Your *raison d'art*, not their shallow *raison d'état*?

Who are you without your vocation, title, or role? How does it feel to simply say, "I am" — and nothing more?

Stop beating the same old drum. Find a new rhythm.

Esse simpliciter sufficit

SPECTRAL

When you pursue your creations and inspirations with unabashed passion and intense focus, you amplify your beneficence to the collective.

When you are "out of your mind," we are granted just a little more space to unwind, co-creating a peaceful, vibrant now.

Love your life

TRANSCENDENCE

We stand at the edge of a profound shift, tethered to the past by the weight of all we've known. As we inch toward transformation, we're caught between the longing for change and the fear of letting go. The world around us mirrors this inner tension, reflecting the battles we fight within. The journey is slow, the resistance palpable, yet it is only by moving through this discomfort that we can awaken to what lies beyond.

. . .

Humanity is in the midst of an etheric housecleaning — a deep clearing of old patterns and energies — yet uncertainty and doubt still keep many submerged. The process is slow and heavy, and too often we paint the present with the same faded palette we used for the past, perpetuating a diminished and defensive mindset.

The world outside mirrors what is happening within. Riots, protests, and sociopolitical unrest are visible manifestations of inner conflict. Many of these disturbances are further inflamed by mass media manipulation, repetitive messaging, and deliberate narratives designed to sow division. The result is a society perpetually out of balance, unconsciously resisting its own ascension, afraid of transcendence and the unknown.

Bound by this mindset, we cling to an intangible idea of control, living in endless cycles of if/then thinking — "if this happens, then I'll be happy" — forgetting that by the time one condition is met, dozens of others will have emerged. Regardless of our deliberations and delays, life moves forward, indifferent to our attempts to hold it still.

Yes, we've been hurt. Hundreds of millions have perished in the past century alone. Yes, we are vulnerable, existing in a volatile realm seemingly biased toward the negative. Yes, we are guilty, ashamed even, knowing we've played a part in the evident chaos. And yet, we've also been played, our humanity — our compassion, trust, and connection — routinely weaponized and turned against us.

But none of this is permanent. Nothing here matters beyond this realm; it serves only the present moment, providing the lessons we need for greater comprehension, discernment, and personal growth. And it is only here and now that we can break free of both imposed boundaries and self-perpetuated limitations.

Life can be more than a cycle of cause and effect, action and reaction. But to transcend it, we must accept our role in the story and confront why we are here. We must step into our creatorship — the authorship of our souls — where sovereignty and purpose merge.

See the facade for what it is: illusions of division, scarcity, and control that keep us small. We are here to move onward and upward, to write and live out the new story — one that reflects our boundless potential and the truth of who we are.

Solvitur ambulando

INFINITE SHAPES OF WATER

The infinite shapes of water
After the rain
Create light-bending splendor
A meditative render
A lively vibrance
Though shaded and gray
Would surely
Make the hidden sun's day

SETTLING UNDONE

In a world that tells us to never settle, we stand at the edge of an endless tug-of-war — independence pulling one way, connection the other. We strive for authenticity but often lose ourselves in self-imposed isolation — afraid to need, afraid to want, afraid to be seen. Navigating our own desires, alongside the desire for another, is not just a personal quest; it reflects a deeper struggle within and around us all.

. . .

"Don't settle; it's better to be alone than to compromise." There's truth in this — and weight. Yet, in refusing to settle, we can become unsettled, retreating into isolation and placing an impossible burden on ourselves: to discern emotional wisdom without the mirror of connection.

As humans, we are not solitary creatures. We are social, interdependent, and spiritual beings. We need communion, objective feedback, and the courage to meet one another with open hearts. But healing, growth, and love often seek the path of least resistance, leading to overcompensation — filling the void with convenience or distractions to avoid the rawness of pain. For the sensitive soul, this means retreating into a carefully guarded emotional landscape, closing off from the unfamiliar.

We resist wanting. We resist needing. In a culture of "I am my own person," traditional partnership is challenged, and our social paradigms shift in response. While this evolution has its benefits, it has also bred confusion and chaos in our relationships.

There's a pervasive lack of emotional maturity in how we connect. Unresolved childhood wounds, unclear boundaries, and generational dysfunction shape our dynamics. Layered atop this is a societal identity crisis — uncertainty about purpose, status, spirituality, sexuality, and progress. In this haze, we struggle to define what we want from a partner or even from ourselves.

And when something stirs our hearts, the barriers we've carefully constructed make us distrust it. The push for individuality and sovereignty mirrors our internal battle, reflecting in the collective turmoil we see around us. What exists "out there" echoes the questions we grapple with "in here."

It's easy to stay cocooned in perceived safety. But life demands expansion, experimentation, and risk. Our hearts, untamed and defiant, call us toward truth, authenticity, and vulnerability. Truth defies stagnation, demanding we live boldly, even if it means scraped knees, bruised egos, or broken hearts along the way.

It's alright to hurt. It's alright to feel deeply, to trust again after the fall, and to risk the pain of loving.

Love, in its most transformative form, unsettles us. It challenges our defenses, strips away our pretenses, and remakes us into something freer, something truer. It calls us to step beyond fear and live — unguarded, wholehearted, alive.

Solvitur ambulando

WEIRDOS

Being a motivator, instigator, spark, inspirer, agitator, uplifter, goader, and heart-connector is your purpose.

Wayshowers aren't bound by existing paradigms or career paths — that's the very essence of their calling. Uplifters earn their keep by embracing their raw, unpredictable, and unapologetically authentic selves.

This is your art. Life is your canvas. Your emotions are the brushes; your thoughts, the paints. The grand gallery is consciousness itself.

You matter. You are needed.

Don't believe everything you think. Old patterns persist only in proportion to the energy we give them.

With every breath, choose love. Keep moving forward.

Sis lux, sis amor, sis tu

LOST

I could have lost myself in you
Willingly
But life doesn't obey lines
And schedules
Never mind all our whims and wants
Paths diverge and wander
As our highest asking is
Always guiding
Silently plotting to maintain beneficence
To the many;
Not disregarding the one, floundering
Frustrated
Bitterly alone
But orchestrating in transcendent tones
The instrumentation
Of the actual
Not practical
Truth…

We think we want what we want
When wants go endlessly unanswered
And substitutes are prostitutes
For our eyes, ears, mind and skin
The cloak and veil so very thin
Anything to placate;
Enervate;
Obfuscate
Obsession

I would have lost myself in you
Unwittingly
But life doesn't feign comfort
As inadequacy persists
It knows my breaking point
Even if I choose to ignore
Pretend it will resolve itself

Not plague me
Forevermore
Shame and blame are today's game
And what is healed in me, I pray
Is loved in you
But only if I am
Willing to
Enter the fire
Divine and unfathomable
To summon the dragon's breath
And purity of the sun
To burn down illusions
Reigniting
The eternal forge...
Silence remains
And your heart
Calls me again

Inadequacy is the Lie

We live in a world that constantly invites us to measure ourselves against external standards — wealth, success, appearance, relationships — yet none of these truly define who we are. These illusions act as mirrors, reflecting the stories we've been told to believe, not the truth of our infinite potential.

. . .

There are countless ways to feel inadequate: career, bank account, body, vocabulary, car, home, friends, community — anything. Outward appearances provide endless fuel for self-doubt and spiritual contraction.

But these so-called realities are mere apparitions, tricks of light. We fool ourselves into believing them, perpetuating the illusion through cultural and social programming. Modern life, with its relentless noise, thrives on keeping us distracted and disconnected. Advertising and consumer culture feed on this disconnection.

It's up to us to stop giving these illusions our life force. When we step back, clarity emerges: what we carry within shapes and frames what we see without.

Yes, connecting the dots of awareness is important — understanding the experiences that sow feelings of inadequacy. But true power lies in the moment we create choice. Life continually reminds us — sometimes subtly, sometimes glaringly — that love is always present, patient, and nonjudgmental, waiting for us to notice.

What persists in our lives reflects what we continue to carry, consciously or unconsciously. We can stay tethered to a victim state, but life offers so much more to those willing to accept, integrate, and move beyond it. The sooner we do, the better, for this earthbound journey is painfully short.

Time and again, we find that when we confront a fear or release a false belief, the truth feels disarmingly simple: "That wasn't so bad." The universe supports whatever we focus on, whether it's anxiety, fear, and futility — or ease, grace, and joy. It's always saying "yes" — the question is, to what?

Every emotion is a signal from our soul, offering fluid and immediate feedback. Each stumble, each setback, is an invitation to look past the mirror and reclaim our truth. Presence in these moments is key.

Inadequacy may feel real, but it is not universal truth. It is an invitation to shed the illusions that obscure who we are.

Let go. Let love.

Temet nosce

Be Willing

Be willing to be with one who fans the fire, quickens the pulse, summons the spirit, focuses the love, cultivates the heart, and defends solace and sovereignty.

Be willing to be this for yourself.

Ardente spiritu, cor in excelsis

The Alchemy of Pain

*Most people mistakenly believe that happiness is the
absence of a load. We want life to be easy, without
challenge or difficulty. However, it is by having a
load that we can have the traction needed to move
forward in our lives.*

— Benjamin Hardy, PhD.

*In a world that teaches us to avoid pain at all costs, we often overlook
a profound truth: it is through struggle and contrast that we grow,
expand, and awaken to our purpose.*

. . .

The avoidance of pain is, paradoxically, its own kind of wounding.
This reality — this life, this planet — is built on contrast, growth,
and exploration. Pain and injury are inevitable, but their impact
depends on how we frame and perceive them.

Our bodies grow stronger through stress and repair: muscles mend
through damaged fibers, bones strengthen through microfractures
and ossification. Force and impact are essential to health. Likewise,
our thoughts and beliefs shape us deeply. We are beings who feel
and reason, propelled toward purpose by the alchemy of conscious
awareness.

We are not automatons. A world devoid of unpredictability would
be lifeless, time itself stagnating. Constriction — whether spiritual,
physical, or psychological — runs counter to our nature. The
struggles we face, though uncomfortable, serve our growth and
curiosity. Why not approach life with wonder? What can we
influence, if not our reactions and perceptions?

This is why we resist control. We cherish autonomy, expression,
and the individuation of experience. Life is a continuous flow of

moments, each one shaping our journey, our humanity, and our legacy.

Our reasons for encountering pain are as varied as we are. Some endure gradual suffering, while others seek extremes, transforming themselves and the world in the process. Our perception of death is key to this journey: it's not the end, but a transition. What matters most is how we live, not how we avoid the inevitable.

Life is creative motion. It listens, leads, and orchestrates the players and circumstances needed to fulfill our desires. When we remember this, pain reveals itself as a catalyst — a doorway to presence, growth, and healing.

Solvitur ambulando

THROUGH THE LENS OF TIME

As we journey through life, our understanding of the past evolves alongside us. With each new layer of experience, we gain the ability to revisit and reinterpret moments that once felt fixed in time — unlocking the power to shift our present, heal old wounds, and embrace a deeper sense of wisdom.

. . .

It's fascinating how our perspectives on past events transform as we grow. Life, with its endless twists and turns, invites us to learn for ourselves, offering countless opportunities to stumble, fall, and rise again — each moment a chance to gain wisdom.

What's particularly intriguing is the concept of time travel within our consciousness. By revisiting past events, we engage with our younger selves, reshaping the lens through which we view those moments. This often subtle and unconscious process integrates greater awareness into our present.

Our memories, inherently fragmented and subjective, can change dramatically. For example, learning something new about a parent or ourselves can reframe an old memory. Suddenly, we see it differently, unraveling layers of meaning we didn't previously grasp. This shift allows us to reimagine the stories we've carried, easing emotional burdens and transforming negative beliefs into understanding and acceptance. It is a form of forgiveness — a profound energy shift that can be life-altering.

The true magic lies in recognizing that the meanings we once assigned to past events were mental constructs shaped by our limited perspectives at the time. The more intense or traumatic the event, the deeper the imprint, though still incomplete. Letting go of outdated perceptions creates space for clarity and lightness. With every release, we invite more freedom into our lives.

As we move forward — individually and collectively — this process accelerates. A small shift in awareness within a critical mass can elevate the collective energy, a rising tide that lifts all boats.

Key moments define our life's trajectory, yet our paths remain fluid, shaped by the choices we make and the beliefs we hold. Moment by moment, our feelings reveal whether we're aligned with our essential truth or drifting from it.

Today, the call is clear: address your hurts and imposed limitations with intention. Create space for your authenticity to emerge.

Do less; imagine more. Talk less; feel more. Work less; adventure more. The journey isn't about becoming someone new but reclaiming more of who you've always been.

Solvitur ambulando

GET REAL CLOSE

Get real close
And you can see
The lines, and spots
The wrinkles, and scars
The salt and pepper
And all those scattered plot points

These raw details
Yours to define

Sometimes they frame
A tired smile;
It's all in the eyes
That sometimes
Lose the pretense
And spill out happiness

This face
Perhaps one of thousands I've worn
Shows me reflecting
All condensed
In this form
Is it new
Or is it some of all
Who were before?
The mirror still frowns
Before I do…

Get real close
And you can see
What might appear
To be
The real me

BE AUTHENTIC

Authenticity isn't just a way of being — it's the gateway to freedom. It liberates the spirit, allowing us to shed the masks we wear and live from the truth of who we really are.

. . .

When you embrace the real you, the noise fades. You might even discover a calmness of spirit you've never known before. It no longer matters where you live, what you drive, what you wear, what's in your bank account, or who you love. You love who you love because they feel like home. That's beautiful. That's courage. That's vulnerability. It's terrifying — and yet, it's exactly what lights up the world.

The world doesn't need you to conform; it needs you to show up. You do what calls to you because that's how you love the world. You push yourself because that's how you honor your potential. Nobody else has the right to define you, control you, or hold you back.

Your baggage? It stays with you until you decide it's time to own it, unpack it, learn from it, transcend it, or let it go. You can take it one step at a time, or you can leap into the unknown and trust yourself to land on your feet. Either way, the path forward is yours alone.

Pay attention to the signals — the spine-straightening tingles, the moments that make you come alive. When you hear that inner call, don't ignore it. Stand tall and say it out loud: *This is my life, this is who I am, and I love it!*

When the world feels too heavy and life seems to close in, pause. Breathe deeply. Gather all the scattered pieces of yourself and bring them here, now. Bring yourself back together. Then, stretch out your heart space. Expand into it. You are safe, and there is nothing to fear.

The heavier the contrast, the brighter the light waiting to emerge behind it. Trust that light. Trust yourself.

That's authenticity: living boldly, loving fully, and showing up for your life as only you can.

Audet vivere vere

Unpredictable and Turbulent

There's a strange thing that happens when we stop resisting the messiness of life. The chaos, the struggle, the unpredictable tides — they're not here to break us. They're here to shape us. Somewhere in the friction, we find our edge, our true selves, and the meaning we've been searching for all along. It's not about avoiding the storm; it's about learning to dance in it.

. . .

You've heard it before: "In these unpredictable and turbulent times..." It's a phrase tossed around in conversations about mindfulness, meditation, and standing up for what we believe in. But isn't it worth asking: does every generation have its own underlying belief in victimhood?

We don't own the rights to struggle, injustice, uncertainty, or political upheaval. These are ancient songs remade, replayed, and revised with updated terminology and shinier technology. Yet, somehow, we adopt a "woe-is-me" stance. Why?

Maybe it's passed down genetically. Maybe it's absorbed from the media we consume, the rituals we follow, the religions we practice, or the traumas we leave unexamined. Perhaps it's something our parents unknowingly taught us. Or maybe it's even written in the stars.

But here's a deeper question: why do we always believe something is wrong — with the world, with others, with ourselves?

Would we know gratitude without lack? Recognize love without hate? Would we even need the word *peace* if we had never known conflict?

We teeter constantly between logic and feeling, distorting the balance like children with a new toy — fascinated one moment, bored or indifferent the next. But these so-called iniquities — the lack, the chaos, the struggle — are essential ingredients in this expansive, fascinating journey. They make life interesting.

The truth is, there are no real victims here. We're all connected by the same creative energy that forms worlds. So why fear danger? Why fear death? In truth, it's not dying we fear — it's regret. The "should-haves" and "if-onlys." We project that fear outward, searching for something or someone to blame for our own lack of courage or awareness.

And yet, let's be honest: we crave the unpredictable. If we didn't, we wouldn't keep coming back for more.

So give yourself some credit. Take time each day to sit with it all — the chaos, the wonder, the uncertainty. Maybe frown. Maybe wonder. And maybe, just maybe, you'll catch yourself smiling.

Because beneath it all, you're a crazy, wonderful, strange human being — here, against all odds, to dance in the storm.

Disce saltare in procellis vitae

KIND-NESS

One of a kind
You, me, them...
Kind of fascinating.
A patient, kind word
Grounding
Compassionate...
All kinds of love;
Life reflects
Respects
Unveils, and unfolds
In kind...

There is no substitute
For kind-ness.

YOU ARE ENOUGH

The tentacles of "not enough" can infiltrate every aspect of our human and spiritual experience. In love, vocation, and purpose, we must cultivate awareness to transcend the lies we've internalized and lived with, regardless of their source.

Temet nosce

NAVIGATING CONTRADICTIONS

We carry unseen weights through life — fears, doubts, and beliefs that were never truly ours. Caught in contradictions, we struggle until we pause long enough to feel the deeper truth beneath the chaos. In this quiet alignment, the true journey begins.

. . .

Life often feels like a tug-of-war between opposing forces, an endless oscillation both within and around us. Like a slow, deliberate metronome, the widest swings create the slowest tempo. Our lives echo this rhythm — ups and downs, where our frequency, our vibration, matters more than the pattern itself.

Heavier energies like fear, resentment, and apathy suppress our playfulness and joy, keeping us tethered to a narrow range of emotion. For some, this is a necessary stage of growth, but for many, it becomes a permanent state — a lifetime spent scratching at an itch for something more, yearning but never reaching.

Even when intuition feels buried, life has a way of nudging us awake. Moments of wonder slip through the cracks. People show up or return, new connections form, and old ones fade. Losses and gains — emotional, financial, or otherwise — disrupt our inertia and rewrite the script. Life challenges our stubbornness, presenting us with the unexpected to draw us forward.

What we inherently seek is steady, engaged presence. When we prioritize external validation, we disconnect from our truth. This erodes trust in our inner guidance and binds us to cycles of shame, blame, and guilt. But as we reclaim our creative energy, we realign with life's natural flow.

Focusing on thoughts that uplift and excite us is a subtle yet powerful shift. It draws us away from people, situations, and beliefs that no longer resonate. This isn't selfishness; it's spiritual integrity.

Walking our path with authenticity allows us to honor ourselves while giving others the freedom to find their way.

Everyone matters. Each of us brings something unique. And the best way to honor both ourselves and others is to follow the lessons, the teachers, and the truths that call most deeply to our hearts. This is the path for navigating contradictions — one step at a time, guided by the steady rhythm of our own alignment.

Love your life

THIS OLD SKIN: PERFECTLY IMPERFECT

We're taught from the start that something is missing — that we must fix ourselves to find peace. But what if the key isn't in perfecting or erasing our flaws, but in embracing them — finding freedom in the beautiful mess of being human?

. . .

Do we have to banish our demons before we can truly live?

The billion-dollar industry of self-help, personal growth, and spiritual awakening often rests on the premise that something is inherently wrong with us. How did this happen? From the moment we're born — before we can reason or even understand words — we're conditioned to believe we're broken. This belief burrows so deeply that it lingers until the day we die, only to reveal, perhaps too late, that it was never true.

I've wrestled with my own shadows, adopting ideas that weren't mine or twisting truths in my search for clarity. These beliefs thrived on the frustrations and confusion I felt about life and the people in it. Yet beneath it all, I've always been driven by a desire to understand and improve the human experience — starting with myself.

Music and words are my chosen mediums, supported by images and an unshakable curiosity about life's mysteries. Feeling my way through it all has always been central to my process. Words often fall short, but perhaps the next song, essay, or conversation will come closer. Isn't that why we sift through countless books, studies, and dialogues — for those rare morsels of wisdom that stick?

But here's the question: since we can never truly "get it done" — not in one lifetime or a thousand — why should we obsess over fixing everything? How could we, in a single fleeting life, possibly be here to save anyone or anything?

166

As a modern culture, we exist in a chaotic, tangled mess. It's maddening and liberating all at once — how wildly and extravagantly we live across the spectrum of human experience. Every size, shape, color, emotion, and disposition is expressed somewhere by someone. It's extraordinary. It's terrifying. It's... eerily perfect.

There's no need to disguise the wounds of the heart, nor should there be. Betrayal cuts deeply and leaves its mark, but it's self-betrayal, self-denial, and self-loathing that we have the power to heal. Through conscious awareness, authentic living, and periodic spiritual upheaval, we can rewrite the stories we tell ourselves. And as we honor ourselves, we naturally learn to honor others.

Life doesn't ask us to conquer fear; it asks us to engage with it. It's not only about "feeling the fear and doing it anyway." It's about feeling the fear, accepting it, and moving forward because something within us dares to explore the unknown — something uncomfortable, challenging, and potentially beautiful.

Because beyond fear lies knowing. And all knowing becomes available... when we're ready.

Solvitur ambulando

THE ART OF FEELING GOOD

We often limit ourselves by defining what we want too narrowly, forgetting that the true essence of our desires lies not in their specifics, but in the feeling they promise to bring.

. . .

The potential trap of specificity is its reliance on a very limited scope of possibility.

Our desired outcomes are shaped by our current mindset and established beliefs. Thus, we benefit from becoming aware of the deeper reasons behind our wants.

A broader, lighter, and more expansive perspective not only frees us from the chronic struggle of figuring out the "hows" but also opens up new paths to what we genuinely want — and even better.

When we show up with openness, inspired action becomes clearer, and the gentle hand of divine guidance is felt intuitively.

Ultimately, the result of everything — and our singular, true desire — is simply feeling good. It's not a specific lover or dollar amount, but acceptance, abundance, creativity, health, gratitude, compassion, self-love, and, of course, happiness.

This is a feeling-based journey, and uncommon sense is paramount.

Love your life

THE BIG PICTURE

We often fall into the trap of thinking our desires are about the "what" — the material, the tangible, the specific. But the truth is, what we seek is far greater than any single thing. It's not about achieving a particular goal; it's about aligning with the expansive, infinite potential already within us.

. . .

Have the audacity to dream big and the courage to be bold. But here's the shift: it's not about material gains — not in the grand scheme. We've been looking at it backward, and now is a perfect time to change perspective.

What's big? What's bold? Love, happiness, excitement — those are big. The universe is big. Consciousness is infinite. Thought is vast. Emotion is profound.

Our days can easily fill with trivialities or the values and priorities others impose upon us. When we get caught up in the smaller aspects of life — fixating on the "how-to" and clinging to every tiny accomplishment — we may become prisoners of small minds and limiting beliefs.

But when we prioritize what truly matters, guided by our core values, we infuse our lives with energy that aligns with our heart's deepest desires. This creates a flow that pulls even the mundane aspects of life toward fulfillment.

Self-discipline becomes natural. Organizing time becomes exciting. Life itself becomes a joyful habit. Even downtime is nourishing because instead of boredom or restlessness, you're dreaming of what's to come, resting easy because your "why" is invigorating.

For too long, we've been unconsciously addicted to the "what-is" — the black-and-white, the struggle for control. Quiet desperation drives us to either overwork ourselves or binge on distractions.

We hide from one another in shame, growing impatient and hypersensitive, instead of cultivating lightness, gratitude, harmony, and untapped joy.

So what's next? Start fresh. Start now. When the chaos of fragmented ideals settles, life boils down to just a few core values we all share: authenticity, compassion, gratitude, growth, and integrity.

Values are what's big. Reconnect with yours. Lay a new foundation. There are countless teachers and guides; listen for the song that resonates with you until you find the courage to sing your own.

Love your life

LIFE'S UNSEEN FLOW

When I step back from the doing and simply observe, the set pieces fall into place, the players move confidently through etheric rehearsal, and the song nearly sings itself.

This grand play demands the full depth of me, yet the tighter I try to grasp the handle, the looser my grip becomes. The play, in its entirety, is the thing — not just one prop, one set, one mistake, one missed or blessed moment, but all of them woven together.

Nothing has meaning except the meaning we give it. Yet it feels hollow without the richness of every breath and every step that brought us here. To discount, deny, or disregard any part of our extraordinary journey is to shortchange the gratitude we seek to embody in moments of joyful ease and hard-won presence.

We may appear to age, to grow, to progress, to achieve; we may believe life continues with or without us. But try to imagine non-existence... My words are nothing without you, the reader.

"Now" is the ever-changing, ever-forming locus of all that is. It cares little for our attempts to confine it with logic or literal definition. All the maths, physics, and spirits inevitably converge into one.

Through presence and authenticity, the flow is realized — even if it's only in flashes. Self-judgment becomes irrelevant. Let go, and let love permeate the hard places while fortifying the soft.

We're well into the second act now, presumably. Bring up the lights. This upcoming scene? It changes everything...

Solvitur ambulando

Three Little Words

I am enough.

The more uncomfortable it feels to say, the more it makes you giggle, brings tears to your eyes, or tempts you to whisper it — the embarrassment, shame, guilt, and everything else it stirs up — the clearer it becomes that you need to hear it, starting now.

You are enough.

THE FIRE WITHIN

We live in a world designed to distract, divide, and diminish our power. Yet the truth is simple: it's always been up to us. Every moment is a choice — how we spend our time, where we direct our energy, and what we decide to believe. The life we've been given is ours to shape.

. . .

Choose your battles wisely. Be deliberate about where and how your time, energy, and attention flow. It's always your choice — no matter the habits or programming you might be tempted to defer to or blame.

Society thrives on weak, low-energy practices meant to keep us fearful, numb, divided, and distracted. We've grown too passive, too gullible, too easily manipulated. Yet, deep down, we yearn to create, to belong, to love and be loved. But when we lack a higher purpose, when we live out of harmony, we default to survival — to behaviors that divide and destroy.

It doesn't have to be this way. Shake things up. Step outside your self-righteousness and question it. Question your cynicism and militance. Examine your fear, worry, and judgment. Question your competitiveness, your ego, your lack of compassion. Challenge your victimhood and martyrdom.

How did I let this happen?

In that moment of raw awareness, let it go.

The desperation, the need to fight — it only summons more fights, more struggles. Whether it's with yourself, your family, "the system," the weeds in your garden, or your own unibrow, the principle is the same.

Use the fire within to burn away impurities. Let the flames create space for clarity, love, and purpose to expand. Stop clinging to the same old wardrobe if you want to refine your style. Start fresh, with naked authenticity.

Why are you hiding?

The real you is vital — here and now, in this chapter of humanity's story. Dive into what makes your heart sing. Surprise yourself. It may not be what you've carried your whole life; it may be something greater.

If you can't enter a fight knowing it ultimately doesn't matter, then you'll keep fighting until you can.

Solvitur ambulando

ANSWER THE CALL

Our greatest challenges and challengers are custom-designed by our greater selves for growth, healing, elevation, evolution, and edification.

Catalysts are our calls to resonance and authenticity.

Answer the call.

A Life à la Carte

We're born into a system that teaches us to survive but not to truly live — to obey, compete, consume, and conform. In the noise and demands, we forget how to simply be. Yet beneath it all, the truth remains: we're here to create, connect, and thrive in ways that honor our essence. This is not a call to action but a call to awareness.

. . .

We ache to reclaim our sovereignty from the psychopathy, insanity, and inanity of post-industrial life. Yet we're terrified of confronting the cycles of lack, struggle, and purposelessness we've clung to for so long. These are just programs — not truths.

Somewhere along the way, we were convinced that performing, consuming, achieving, out-thinking, and conforming were the ultimate ideals. But if that's true, why do we grow more desperate, isolated, and anxious with each passing year?

We've been persuaded that the "I" holds all the value, while "we" is a distant, secondary concern. My car, my house, my bank account, my children, my legacy, my retirement. My ignorance.

We've reduced ourselves to selfish, servile, monotone creatures, clamoring in a chaos of suppression. So much truth is buried — filed away, distorted, hidden.

The heaviness is palpable, especially in our cities. We walk past the hungry and forgotten, tossing half our industrially-produced food into the trash. We avoid eye contact, shielding ourselves from their shame — and from them seeing our own. We shy away from heartful connection to protect the lies we tell ourselves.

To what end?

"Happiness is a choice," they say. Forget that. It's not even on the menu anymore. It's been blended into a concoction of maligned ideas and overcomplicated offerings. Give me life à la carte.

Enough with the competition, callousness, insensitivity, and egoistic grandstanding. Enough with the selling, shouting, and forcing.

Life is a simpler song — written in the heart's uncommon rhythms, with a melody that serves the soul. It waits in the stillness, present in our calm.

It's in a child's eyes, a father's laughter, a mother's smile. It hides in the forest, dances in the river, and is reborn in the sea.

We all have access to life's ingredients. We can choose to create something healthier, something whole, nourishing, and deeply satisfying.

It's time to shed this existential weight — this collective burden — with passion, empathy, authenticity, courage, and love. Only together can we rise above this illusion of separation.

Be the truest version of yourself. Look me in the eye, and together, let's dare greatly.

Esse, non conformari

PRETTY SOON

Pretty soon
Our eyes will adjust
To the wider spectrum
But not before our hearts
Do their parts

Truths and reality
Much broader than
We're trained to see
As the universe exposes
Right under our noses
That which always was
Before we took
To forgetting

Make dear
What you fear
To rise above
And include it
Diffusions of
Illusions are
Dated
Overrated
Enervated
And spent

Now... is now
Forever;
Come home

ON BECOMING: SMALL STEPS

Life is a journey, not just a destination. Yet, we often get distracted by battles that drain our creative energy. When we focus on our deeper desires and take small, inspired steps daily, the process itself transforms us. It's not about hustling or waiting for motivation — it's about showing up with presence, passion, and play.

. . .

What's your trajectory? What do you truly desire in life? Too often, we drain ourselves battling over petty distractions, losing sight of what really matters. We are passionate, adventurous creators, equipped with limitless energy waiting to be accessed as we clear the noise and reconnect with presence.

Many of us struggle with ego, confusion, and disconnection from purpose. We hesitate, avoid discomfort, or let external pressures hold us back. But the real work — honoring our original creative impulse — is the journey itself.

Begin with the most grounding thought: "I am enough." Remind yourself daily — upon waking and before sleep — until it truly sets in. This isn't just an affirmation; it's a declaration. Stand confidently in your God-given power, knowing creation is conspiring with you.

From this foundation, take inspired action. Move your body, clear the clutter, and align your energy with what you desire. Recognize that beyond attraction lies acceptance: when what you seek arrives, will you see and embrace it, or let doubt hold you back? Self-sabotage is the result of old programming — rise above it.

Take one step each day toward your desires. Practice — whether writing, painting, training, or problem-solving — builds the path. Each action, no matter how small, reshapes you into the version of yourself ready to receive and appreciate what you want.

Progress comes faster than you think. The elements and co-creators you need are already out there, waiting for your alignment. This isn't about exhausting yourself — though for some, the struggle may be their refiner's fire. Success looks different for everyone, but we all possess the latent ability to tap into limitless source energy.

Here's a tip: do what you hate first. Clear the unpleasant tasks to make space for flow. Make mistakes. Make many mistakes. Don't wait for motivation — life is too short. Sometimes, you'll find yourself loving what you once dreaded.

Our creative nature is often buried under layers of conditioning. The key is awareness — choosing, moment by moment, to anchor yourself in a deeper knowing. We are greater than we suppose ourselves to be.

Life is simple. Love is simple, too. Ultimately, we all want to feel good, to be happy — not just occasionally, but consistently. It's time to turn the page and start fresh, straight from the heart.

Solvitur ambulando

The Climb

From the moment our dreams first take shape in childhood, they are pure and untainted by the obstacles life later imposes — yet it is only by reconnecting with that original inspiration that we can truly climb the mountains we are meant to ascend.

. . .

The uphill battle is always our own figurative mountain. The dreams and aspirations that emerge in childhood are closest to our hearts because life has yet to "get in the way."

The longer we wait to engage with our purest inspiration, the further down the slope we may slide. Life works with us or against us only as much as we choose; it is the ever-willing partner in whatever arena we dare to enter — or avoid.

It does not judge; the universe is only ever a resounding "yes!"

Time is irrelevant. Worry is irrelevant. The question "But, how?" is irrelevant.

Nothing flickers across our consciousness without our inherent capacity to fulfill it. While our mind may perceive only one path, one result, one outcome, it's not for our mind to discern the how, the who, the where, or the when. *It's the why.*

Beyond mere material gains, the why is always to feel good; to feel happy; to feel that we are being of service — to our spirit, our purpose, and to the human collective.

Start with the heart. Follow your feet. Keep your eyes open.

Solvitur ambulando

DISSIPATING THE FOG

It surrounds
Confounds
Stays so close
Familiar yet unfriendly

If there is an artist's way
Surely it resides
Outside of this…
This prevailing heavy

Eyes lowered
Spirits shy
Tempers triggered
Every night
Press an impression
On the mind
Dress the concession
Left behind

Truth!
Why are you oscillating from view?
Oh, that's me swinging right past you

Small wonder the fog persists

Yet every time I reach
And trip
And fall
We're face
To face

I see it all

TRUE STRENGTH

True strength lies in embracing your authentic self, and in recognizing that independence doesn't mean isolation — it means being whole within, so you can show up fully for yourself and others.

. . .

Be your own source of strength. Be wholly and powerfully you, so you don't depend on anyone else — not your partner, spouse, or would-be lover.

But really, why?

Are you conforming to a culturally accepted version of independence, toughening up to foster resilience, grit, and stature? Or are you being truly honest with yourself about your fundamental needs?

Emotional needs are real. That doesn't make you needy.

You are not a soulless machine, designed to function without connection or care. You are organic — a distinctive blend of soul and the imprints of life itself. You are a sovereign spirit, an intensely focused individuation of the eternal, loved without question.

But right here, right now, you are an explorer. And while nothing can harm the greater you, there are volatile energies, malevolent entities, and nefarious agendas that feed off your forgetting.

The idea that you must isolate yourself to forge personal power and emotional resilience might harm you more than help. Vulnerability is not a weakness.

Our society's obsession with hero worship — and worship in general — is an insidious poison, rooted in runaway masculine energies. We're stumbling back toward balance, but the path isn't easy. The greatest challenge lies in dropping false fronts, shedding the massive weight of pretense, and abandoning the illusion that safety and security can be forced through sheer will.

Your deep truth, your essence — your creator substance — doesn't care for masks or performances. Pretense only smudges and blurs your genuine colors.

You are not alone. Not ever. You are always held, always loved. Let go of the fear that connection makes you weak. True strength is found in openness, in the courage to be seen and to see others without walls.

Keep your heart open. It's your greatest compass and the truest source of power you will ever know.

Simul potentiores

Enchanted Sol

When the time is right...
You'll forget all the tasks
The myriad asks
And the moments they took

Because you're still here
That bright golden sphere
Ignites you with only a look

ON CHANGE: RIDING THE WAVE

Change is no longer a distant possibility — it's here, crashing toward us like an unstoppable wave. Resistance only drains us. The real challenge is learning to ride it. Pain will accompany this shift, but rather than being an enemy, it is the fire that refines us, pushing us toward deeper authenticity and strength.

. . .

You can resist all you want, but the wave is already upon us. Radical change defines our time, and learning how to surf it is our only choice. Try to duck-dive through it, and you'll only exhaust yourself. Pain is inevitable — a constant companion and impartial teacher. Like love, it demands that we pay attention, challenging us to grow in both mind and body.

But don't believe the commercial promises of relief. Don't let them sell you the illusion of escape, and never simply "ask your doctor," because what they're pushing solves nothing. This pain isn't a mistake; it's been invited. It's here to shake loose the stagnant, the stale, and the false. Without pain, without change, we wither, hastening our own decline.

As we collectively navigate this profound transition — this housecleaning of the soul of the world, this stripping down to the core — we are being called to a new level of self-awareness and deeper self-respect. The old ways of tolerating nonsense, settling for less, and endlessly compromising will no longer suffice.

So, turn the page and keep writing the new story, inside and out. Expect chaos. Let it terrify you — and invigorate you. The fire cannot harm what is real, what is authentic, or what is truly alive.

Invicta in tempestate

YOUR LIVING STORY

Every life is a story, unfolding one moment at a time. Yet, too often, we overlook the significance of our own narrative, distracted by regrets of the past or the pull of an uncertain future. The truth is, the most powerful chapters are written in the present — where our choices, our presence, and our courage come alive.

. . .

Look around. This is your life.

Whatever you think of it — however you measure, judge, or attempt to define it — the days have passed, the pages have turned, and here you are.

If you were to write an autobiography, what moments would you highlight? What achievements, pivotal events, or defining choices would you include? Would there be pages marked with an asterisk for future reflection or significance? Or would you struggle to name those moments, unsure of what truly stands out? It's not uncommon for self-worth to obscure our ability to see the value in our own story.

Regrets, unrequited love, failures, missed opportunities — these tend to dominate our recollection, carrying a weight that drains our energy and scatters it across the fragments of a life we cannot change. They pull us away from the only place where our presence truly matters: here and now, the very locus of our creative power.

The past, however, need not be a prison. Viewed through the right lens, it becomes a mirror — revealing how it has shaped you, how it informs your choices, perpetuates assumptions, and perhaps nudges you toward greater awareness and authenticity.

Healing the fractures of your spirit and progressing through them is no small task. It might take a lifetime. But within that journey lies something extraordinary: a story only you can write, a narrative no one else can claim.

To ignore it, to dismiss its worth, is to deny the essence of who you are.

Scribe vitam tuam

YOU ARE GOOD

Life will always build bridges and roads from you, to you.

You can venture far into the depths, or across time and dimensions, yet upon arriving (or returning?), you find more of yourself.

And now, you see more. You are more whole.

> *You are good when you are one with yourself.*
> *Yet when you are not one with yourself you are not*
> *evil.*
> *For a divided house is not a den of thieves; it is only*
> *a divided house.*
> *And a ship without rudder may wander aimlessly*
> *among perilous isles yet not sink to the bottom.*

— Kahlil Gibran, from *The Prophet*

THE RAIN AND THE SUN

I do miss the rain
But I do love the sun
What's with me again
Was never undone

Storms come and go
Moving earth moving dust
The flesh doesn't know
In what feelings to trust

I do miss the rain
But I do love the sun

THE BATTLE WITHIN

In the midst of our internal battles, the answers often elude us — but sometimes, it's in the uncertainty itself where the journey begins.

. . .

Our battles are ours alone. The swirl of external circumstances may challenge or shape us, but the war is always within.

I don't know what the hell to do.

And that's a good place to start. It's raw. It's real. It's the truth of you breaking through the chaos, cracking the polished facade. You don't have to know what to do — not all the time.

For ages, our culture has fixated on doing, endlessly subverting deeper aspects of our humanity to sustain a system built on productivity, sustenance, and economy.

Where are the ancient tales of great banks, corporations, mortgages, and concrete? Do tribal leaders, chiefs, gurus, priests, shamans, or storytellers gather around to recount those? *Hell no.*

The oldest stories are about life's essence: love, art, myths, and legends; battles, ascension, and spiritual transformation. They're about shapeshifting, mastering the elements, dancing with nature spirits, and honoring family.

We've carried lies within us for so long that we question our sanity — but rarely do we question the constructs that gave rise to the insanity. We guard our little spaces and collections of things so fiercely that we've forgotten the greater cohesion, the source of all that is, leaving us to believe we're insignificant, separate, and small.

No. I don't know what the hell to do.

But I can feel. I can hurt, now and again — for myself and for you. Resolve comes not through avoidance but through feeling: the ache, the stagnation, the frustration, even the madness.

Through it all, I welcome the beautiful retrospective, the cleaner slate, the naked canvas.

Solvitur ambulando

Not So Gone

Gone, perhaps, but the story goes on —
In the forest, what seems dead
gives life to critters and bugs,
a home for birds,
a partner for the wind's quiet dance,
a refuge for shadows to hide
from the sun and moonlight

In winter, it rests,
and I, too, pause —
reflecting on this new chapter
in a peaceful, snowy field

Not so gone, after all

DANCING WITH EVERYTHING

We stand at the crossroads of possibility, where every moment hums with potential — yet we're caught in the tide of time, constantly pulled between what is and what could be. It's easy to be swept away, but if we pause, we might catch a glimpse of something deeper — the quiet, ever-present force that guides us beyond the noise.

. . .

We live in an era of relentless flux, massive change, and energetic upheaval — a reality that takes its toll on both seasoned veterans and the uninitiated. Our minds can become a veritable soup, stirred by the daily inundation of inner and outer influences.

How, then, can we find clarity of purpose, presence, and trust in the flow? Life's busyness and business can be utterly unforgiving — unapologetically brash in their demands.

Much of this chaos is by unconscious design, but much of it is also intentional. Problems arise, challenges are perceived, and solutions devised — yet we often operate on symptomatic premises rather than addressing systemic truths. Conditioned to think linearly, we react rather than embracing our most natural state of consciousness: fluid, timeless, ever-evolving.

Today's concerns are often fabricated or deliberately exaggerated, exploiting our raw and vulnerable states. Those disconnected from nature profit by fueling our cravings for superficial distractions, transient desires, and fleeting fears. This cycle has persisted for millennia, but now, more than ever, we are awakening to its presence and learning to discern its influence.

Through the empowerment of knowing, we begin to see how new information triggers us. And we must remember: our perceptions are just that — perspectives. Nothing more. Our initial reactions are often only the tip of the perceptual iceberg.

Let whatever arises come up. Love it, unravel it, and use it. Don't assume that the outer packaging is all there is to learn, see, or understand. The pearl may require effort to liberate and consciously integrate.

It is *all* available to us. Our imaginings, no matter how fantastical, exist as pure potentiality if they are genuine, authentic, and relevant. They dare us — to persist, to find courage, and to show up fully in the present, ready to make them manifest.

Trip, stumble, and fall. Then trip, stumble, and fall again. But let each misstep reveal its lesson, each challenge its hidden gift. Laugh in the face of it all, because what seems like chaos at first is merely the beginning of understanding.

What appears as prose in the moment becomes poetry when seen in its fullness. And within that poetry lies the quiet, ever-present force — the dance of everything, guiding us back to ourselves.

Love your life

A QUIET PLACE

A quiet place, lonely but never truly alone.

This divine life offers infinite variety, if only we're willing to embrace it. Yet, persistent sadness too often mires the spirit and silences the adventurer.

I've certainly lingered there.

Never let curiosity be stifled for too long. It's true — pain often teaches more than play. There's a quiet courage in facing hurt again and again, but that's far from life's totality — even if originality sometimes eludes us.

I've certainly wrestled with that.

A scraped knee, a battered heart, an exhausted mind… It's naïve to think we'd escape unscathed. But perhaps the goal isn't to throw in the towel — it's to use it: to wipe the sweat from our brow and the blood from our lips.

A quiet place, inevitably.

I'm learning your secrets.

OUTSIDE OF ENMITY

Life offers itself to us in whispers and storms, in ripe fruit and empty branches. The journey inward — where truth, love, and the essence of who we are resides — often begins only when we stop reaching for what isn't ready and allow ourselves to simply be.

. . .

It doesn't matter whom I want to help, heal, or love if I can't first embody and extend those things to myself. This divine, earthbound journey carries us through an orchard of endless abundance, yet we often grasp at unripe fruit — whether out of vanity or innocence — and then wonder why bitterness lingers.

Everything unfolds in its time and place.

The pain, the resistance, the tension, the enmity — these are our teachers, though they rarely announce themselves as such. And love? Love is the ever-present force, the gentle monster that never leaves your side. It is you, in entirety, holding infinite space, indifferent to inessentials, trivialities, and our concept of time.

It urges you, again and again, to listen more intently, to feel with greater depth. It calls for daring, willingness, wonder, and the critical realization that the tightrope you believe you're walking is an illusion, held aloft by mere perception.

How often do we sever our extraordinary abilities, aspirations, heart murmurings, and lifelong passions because we've been taught not so much to question, but to distrust? Cynicism has its moments, but release it before it poisons you.

Beyond enmity lies pure potential. Perhaps what we need most is a simple mantra: *Be easier on yourself.*

Temet nosce

PATTERNS IN THE STORM

There's a space within each of us, quiet and still, where everything we've ever sought resides. It's easy to overlook, buried beneath layers of noise and distraction, but it's always there — waiting, patient, like the pulse of the earth beneath our feet. We wander far, we search wide, but the greatest journey is the one within.

. . .

There is much suffering here, and for sensitive souls and creatives, it often strikes harder and deeper.

You don't have to go looking for it. You don't have to "heal the world," because much of what you see outside is a projection of what is being processed within.

When we are young, we carry a heightened energetic state, a vibrant imprint of the spacetime we entered. As we age, the weight of generational imprints and accumulated heaviness settles in, layering itself over our essence.

Life doesn't pause for this recalibration. It continues relentlessly, even amid the emotional storms, upheavals, and swings across the spectrum of experience.

It's tempting to escape. A mountain retreat, a serene beach, a sacred shrine — or a spa filled with therapeutic reprieve, both practical and esoteric — might seem like the ideal answer. But for most of us, these sanctuaries are occasional luxuries at best, unattainable dreams at worst.

So, what do we do?

We try to smoke it away, dose it away, or numb it with substances. It doesn't work.
We escape through entertainment, constant busyness, or frenetic travel, creating chaos to drown the noise within. It doesn't work.

We suppress by starving ourselves — physically, emotionally, spiritually — feeding the cycle of want, lack, and emptiness, as though penance were a solution. It doesn't work.

We oppress through rigid control — of others, of our environment, even of our own emotions and expectations. We withhold love, deny intimacy, and grow callous. It doesn't work.

You see the pattern. Much of modern life is shaped by these distortions and imbalances, and we are in the throes of bringing it all to the surface.

It all needs to be processed — patiently, consciously, and with a discerning eye for patterns. This is where our innate gifts come into play.

We are born healers, carriers of an essence that is pure and abundant. Within us is a space that always has enough, always says, *Yes, I know. Let's face this together.*

Be gentler with yourself. Unconditional love surrounds you, ready to meet you where you are. Help arrives as openly as you are willing to receive it.

Solvitur ambulando

TRUST TAKES TIME

There's a quiet chaos within each of us — a web of contradictions and untold stories. It's often in the spaces between those contradictions that we begin to understand ourselves. We wear our wounds like badges, but it's in their unraveling that we find the thread of who we truly are.

. . .

Yes, we need to trust our internal emotional guidance system, but we can only trust it to the degree that we are aware of ourselves.

Which aspect of you is reacting to this?

Is it the one that's been shattered — where trust was destroyed, leaving everything numb and disconnected?

Is it the one you inherited from a parent, teaching you to see things as strictly good or bad?

Is it the one that feels guilty for moving toward something that feels good?

Is it the one that's ashamed — of your appearance, your bank account, your old car, your sensitive nature, or your bold and brutally honest way of expressing yourself?

We are many pieces, yet we are one.

A book has many chapters, far beyond the back-cover summary or the blurb on the first page. To truly know who you are, you must acquaint yourself with the many aspects that make you whole. Some might call this recapitulation — a process of life review. This awareness is the key to integrating and elevating your understanding of self, which is essential for authentic connection and communication, both within and with others.

Our thoughts and feelings don't necessarily belong to us, yet we often attach our sense of self to them, getting swept away on the energetic rollercoaster they create.

These elements — our emotions, thoughts, and reactions — are constantly shaped by inner and outer forces: the people around us, our environment, the sounds we hear, our health, diet, exercise, routines, and, perhaps most importantly, our breathing patterns.

Trust, whether in ourselves or in others, takes time and practice.

So, be gentler with yourself.

Confide in te ipso

The Whole World

We've built our world inside a tiny box. We call it progress — this civilization of economies, technologies, treaties, and trade. We've been sold the idea that this box defines who we are, what we're worth, and what we're meant to do. But this box is not the whole world. It's not even close.

. . .

Your country, your continent, the entirety of civilization under current systems of economy, treaties, banking, trade, and technology — none of it is the whole world.

Today, you can hold the "world" in your hand through a smartphone. But are you truly experiencing it? That five-inch screen delivers only a version of reality. Rely on it too heavily, and you're left with little more than eye strain, neck pain, and the illusion of understanding, comprehension, and connection.

The more you buy into the oppressive idea that life is defined by technology, commerce, money, mining, wars, progress, and plastic surgery, the more you cloud your judgment. You begin to mistake ignorance for truth, becoming lost in the cogs of the machine. You end up buying things you don't need, believing politicians, thinking you can poison yourself into health, and suffering from spiritual sabotage — all while acting out as an emotionally stunted adult child.

But here's the truth: What is most real, most true, lies beyond words, beyond calculation, beyond all the things we try to control.

If you think you know what love is, even the mention of it should stop you in your tracks. Love can't be commodified, quantified, labeled, or packaged. It can't be boxed with greeting cards, chocolates, or plastic wrap. All of that is just a superficial, commercial attempt to limit the infinite.

The world is far bigger than the small box we've built for ourselves.

The question is: What will you choose?

You choose your diet, your education, your environment, your sources of information, and your cognitive biases. You choose your present, your future, and yes — your figurative and literal wounds. You choose to heal and to harm, again and again. You choose whether to be hardened by it all... or not.

This world is more expansive, richer, and more vibrant than we're ever told. Go beyond the limits of the box. See it for what it is. Love it for what it offers. Live it fully. Give yourself to it without hesitation.

Let the old you fall away, again and again. Step into the fire and recognize the flames as your own. What burns away was never truly you. What remains is what always was: pure, unbounded, alive.

Keep your eyes open. The whole world is waiting.

Love your life

About the Author

Trance Blackman is a writer, artist, and seeker of truth whose work reflects a profound commitment to amplifying the light and inspiring transformation. Blending poetry, poetic prose, reflective essays, and bold perspectives, his writing invites readers to navigate life's complexities with courage and authenticity — to question the status quo, uncover deeper truths, and embrace the vibrant beauty of their unique journey.

Trance's creative path spans the sonic landscapes of music, the visual storytelling of photography and media production, and the introspective world of writing. His work resonates with dreamers and seekers, offering a voice to those ready to move beyond the superficial and into the depths of what is real, meaningful, and true.